UNDERSTANDING THE BIBLE

UNDERSTANDING THE BIBLE

AN INTRODUCTION FOR SKEPTICS, SEEKERS, AND RELIGIOUS LIBERALS

JOHN A. BUEHRENS

BEACON
150

BEACON PRESS
BOSTON

Beacon Press
Boston, Massachusetts
www.beacon.org

Beacon Press books
are published under the auspices of
the Unitarian Universalist Association of Congregations.

20 19 18 17   8 7 6

This book is printed on acid-free paper that meets
the uncoated paper ANSI/NISO specifications
for permanence as revised in 1992.

"O tell us, poet," by Rainier Maria Rilke from *Later Poems*
translated by J. B. Leishman and published by The Hogarth Press.
Used by permission of St. John's College, Oxford, and
The Random House Group Limited.

Excerpts from "Advice to a Prophet" in
Advice to a Prophet and Other Poems, copyright 1959 and
renewed 1987 by Richard Wilbur, reprinted by permission of Harcourt, Inc.

Text design by Dean Bornstein

Composition by Wilsted & Taylor Publishing Services

Library of Congress Cataloging-in-Publication Data
Buehrens, John A.
Understanding the Bible : an introduction for skeptics,
seekers, and religious liberals / John A. Buehrens.
    p.   cm.
Includes bibliographical references.
ISBN 0-8070-1052-9 (cloth)
ISBN 0-8070-1053-7 (pbk.)
1. Bible—Introductions. I. Title.
BS475.3.B84 2003
220.6'1—dc21
                  2003001438

*To fellow seekers for understanding
who have joined me on the journey that made this book*

Happy are those who find wisdom,
And those who get understanding.

PROVERBS 3:13

If the Bible is a flaming sword
forbidding our entrance to the garden,
it is also a burning bush urging us toward freedom.
It is what we wrestle with all night
and from which we may,
if we demand it,
wrest a blessing.

ALICIA SUSKIN OSTRIKER

Philip . . . heard him reading the prophet Isaiah. He asked,
"Do you understand what you are reading?"
He replied, "How can I, unless someone guides me?"

ACTS 8:30-31

CONTENTS

BEFORE WE BEGIN

Reasons: Why Bother with the Bible?

❧ ❧ ❧ ❧

"An intelligent understanding of the Bible is indispensable to anybody in the Western world who wishes to think wisely about religion. By no possibility can any one of us be independent of the Bible's influence. Our intellectual heritage is full of its words and phrases, ideas and formulas. Ignorance of it constitutes a hopeless handicap in the endeavor to understand any great Western literature."[1]

The great liberal minister Harry Emerson Fosdick wrote those words in 1925. They are just as true today. The influence of the Bible remains pervasive in our culture. It not only functions as authoritative scripture for our largest religious communities, both Christian and Jewish. Its language and stories also still resonate throughout our literature and public rhetoric. Many contentious political debates in our public life — over issues of sexuality, economics, even foreign policy — disguise sharply divergent interpretations of the Bible.

My friend Forrest Church is the son of the late U.S. senator Frank Church of Idaho. In his book *God and Other Famous Liberals: Reclaiming the Politics of America*, Forrest argued that the Bible and God, like the Constitution and the American flag, like Motherhood and Apple Pie, remain powerful icons in our culture. Progressive people simply cede their power to opponents when they leave interpretation of our religious heritage, or the meaning of our nation, or authentic "family values," to the reactionaries, the chauvinists, and the bigots. Bishop John Spong of the Episcopal Church has similarly called for *Rescuing the Bible from Fundamentalism*. Like Fosdick, both are ministers who see biblical fundamentalism and literalism for what they truly are: not authentic faith, but disguised fear; reactions against modernity that violate the Bible's own spirit, and even its guideline of how it should be interpreted: "For the letter kills, while spirit gives life" (cf. Rom. 2:27 and 7:6; 2 Cor. 3:6).

Oppressive interpretations of the Bible do kill, literally. You'll find no denial of that here. Massive injustice has been and continues to be done in the name of the Bible. But the problem is not simply with or within religion. The problem is that all of us allow the powers and principalities of both secular and spiritual oppression to usurp the spirit of the Bible and use it to legitimize such clear sins as economic and environmental exploitation, racism, sexism, homophobia, and more. Meanwhile the Bible is also about the beauty and goodness of creation itself; about the ancient human struggle for freedom and liberation; about frustration with violence and injustice throughout the generations; and about experiences of exultation, expectation, and inspiration that can sustain the human quest for wisdom, justice, and peace. Understood properly, it is also a remarkably honest look at the true religious spirit itself being taken captive, even crucified, by hierarchies of church and state, and at the perennial need to resurrect and renew a true discipleship of equals.

Perhaps because we sense all this at some level, most people who own books at all own at least one Bible, if only an inherited one. Sales of new Bibles have never been greater. Yet surveys show that the reading and the study of the Bible has markedly declined—among all groups except the very fundamentalists who would take its words most literally. The results are deeply ironic. Today many otherwise well-informed, intelligent people—religious liberals, seekers after wisdom and justice, even skeptics and the news media—often speak as though the Bible says and means only what those fundamentalists say that it says and means!

This shows not only a lack of understanding but also a failure of maturity and wisdom. Those who reject or neglect the Bible fail to recognize that to "throw the Bible out" because others have turned it into an idol, or because you don't accept what you take to be the conventional understanding of its teachings, doesn't mean that it ever goes away. Rather it simply means that it ends up only in the hands and on the lips of others—often reactionary others—where it can and will be used against you.

Take my friend Debra Haffner. She is a leading sexuality educator and advocate for sane, responsible, justice-oriented approaches to human sexuality. While serving as head of SIECUS, the Sexuality Information and Education Council of the United States, she became eligible for a sabbatical leave. "I need to study the Bible," she told me. "It's being used against everything I know to be true, just, and healthy. Where do I begin?" When I suggested a progressive seminary for religious study, one thing just led to another and she is now the Reverend Debra Haffner!

Not all of us, however, can or should go to seminary to begin to take back our right to read and interpret the Bible for ourselves. We can begin with a basic book like this one, and with a little self-examination. Since there is justice-seeking in the Bible, and surely some spiritual truth that has managed to endure through the ages, how did we happen to give away our right to question religious authority and to interpret the Bible for ourselves?

The late Rabbi Abraham Joshua Heschel, a great champion of social justice, had a theory. We tend to misdirect our skepticism, he said. We use it to ask superficial questions of the Bible, like "Is this story really, historically true?" (Another great Bible scholar quipped that many Bible stories are not literally true — just eternally true!) Instead of directing our skepticism toward our forebears, maybe we should direct some toward ourselves, Heschel said. Is it possible that we use our superficial questions to avoid more important ones in the Bible? Questions like those posed by the prophet of old: "What does the Lord require of you, but to do justice, to love mercy, and to walk humbly with your God?" (Mic. 6:8). Is it possible that we have turned away from eternally important questions because we are uncomfortable with the idea that the Eternal, the God of history, actually might require something from us? Is that why we have replaced that question with the more comfortable questions of a consumerist age: "What do I require?" Require in a book, a teaching, a God, or a good that I might be willing to take seriously.

So one reason to bother with the Bible today has to do with questions of justice and power. Another has to do with sheer cultural literacy.

In Fosdick's generation, and even Heschel's, it could be assumed that most American young people had been taught something of the Bible. As children they had lessons from it at home or in church. Even in the public schools of many communities, daily Bible readings were still the

norm well into the 1950s, sixties, and beyond. Some had at least studied the Bible "as literature" in college or private school. Many others
had been in adult Bible classes at church, if only in the more traditional
congregations they began in, not the more liberal ones they went to after they started raising critical questions about it.

Today, however, many people will admit to having little real understanding of the Bible. This is true even for members of justice movements that were inspired by the progressive biblical interpretations
of earlier generations. It is true today even in progressive schools and
congregations. Many people are vaguely aware of at least some recent
developments in biblical studies — archeological discoveries, historical
studies, insights from comparative religion and anthropology, liter-
ary/critical or feminist interpretations. But there are relatively few accessible, popular books available to summarize these developments and
help people with a basic, up-to-date understanding of the Bible. Those
that do exist often seem aimed at believers, or defending or "rescuing"
the Bible.

So to many who are not about to give up their sense of disquietude
and suppressed questioning about the Bible, there are few guides available except collections of literary essays, scholarly treatises, and seminary textbooks, or an endless stream of pious books aimed at those who
consider themselves "Bible believers."

This volume is addressed to the rest of us — skeptics, seekers after
justice and wisdom, and religious liberals. I began writing it shortly after the horrifying attacks of September 11, 2001. Bookstores were reporting that sales of the Koran had soared. Clearly many thoughtful
people were desperately trying to find some understanding of events
and of Islam from examining its scriptures. Given the highly poetic nature of the Koran — and how hard it would be to discern where its
versions of stories in the Bible differ from those in the Hebrew and
Christian scriptures — I suspect that most Korans were soon set aside
in frustration.

I'm reminded of a parody hymn that a friend of mine once penned.
It's to be sung to the tune of "Onward Christian Soldiers," which has
another, more liberal, set of words: "Forward through the Ages." His
parody goes this way: "Forward through the pages/ Never read a line./

Honor all the scriptures,/ Think them all just fine./ Books of differing sizes/ Spread across our shelves;/ We will never read them;/ We think for ourselves!"[2]

When I was in college, many of the most interesting friends I made had been raised in progressive homes that had far more books on the shelves than the home in which I had been raised. They were morally engaged in the issues of the time. But they were biblically and religiously ignorant. Because I was majoring in Renaissance and Reformation studies and had at least some religious literacy, they often turned to me to explain the biblical and religious references in paintings, poems, and other texts — even in jokes!

Like the one about Dorothy Parker arriving at a New York apartment for a swank party, clad in her little basic black dress with pearls. A young actress, dressed to the nines, arrived at the door at the same moment. There was a certain jockeying for precedence. Finally the young actress stepped back, saying, "Well, age before beauty, I suppose!" Going ahead, Dorothy Parker reportedly quipped, "No, my dear: pearls before swine!" Writer and raconteur Isaac Asimov once sadly reported that he had decided to stop telling that joke, because fewer and fewer people seemed to get the biblical reference anymore![3]

Even among erstwhile, cultured despisers of the Bible, however, the tide may be turning. There is a growing yearning for an understanding of the biblical heritage that is intellectually respectable, justice-oriented, and spiritually enriching. I can testify to that.

When I was serving a liberal, activist congregation in the very secular city of New York during the late 1980s I gave a series of lectures that eventually gave rise to the book you have before you. It was striking to me how many people of great sophistication were drawn to those lectures. When they were over, a group of women writers and educators surprised me even more by coming to me, asking if I would meet with them for a closer study of selected portions of the Bible, every week. I was both stunned and gratified.

At first they claimed that their motivations were related to their craft as writers and people of culture. They knew that no one can claim to be culturally literate without an understanding of the Bible, since it has influenced, directly or indirectly, nearly all of Western literature and art. The literary critic Northrop Frye argued this well in his book *The Great Code: The Bible and Literature*. Not only is it obvious that one can't fully understand Renaissance art, Bach, Shakespeare, Milton, T. S. Eliot, or even Emily Dickinson, without understanding the "coded" biblical references and their interpretations. It is also true that even many modern writers and artists in rebelliion against the standard interpretations of the Bible and its authority can only be understood against the backdrop of what they reject. Biblical themes are also a source of continuing inspiration and creativity for novelists, poets, and artists. Not to mention for ordinary people struggling for justice and seeking an authentic and deeper wisdom, maturity, and spirituality. And as our group study of the Bible went along, that became a third important motivation.

The first motivation could be called political: If you can't or won't understand the Bible, others surely will interpret it for you. The second could be called cultural or literary: Within this culture you can't be fully literate or creative, artistically or rhetorically, without an acquaintance with the Bible. But now we come to the third and most personal reason: You also can't be spiritually mature or wise by simply rejecting the Bible as oppressive. The oppressive uses of the Bible are real, but unless you learn to understand that there are other readings possible, the Bible will, indeed, simply continue to be a source of oppression for you, and not a source of inspiration, liberation, creation, and even exultation as you understand it anew for yourself, at a deeper and less literal level.

Some people have to go quite far in rejecting the Bible before they ever discover this. Still another of my friends rejected his Christian upbringing and its theology as a young adult and spent five years in Japan studying Zen Buddhism, only to have his Buddhist teacher send him back to the Bible. Life is short, he told him, and he might have time to become a good Buddhist in his next incarnation. In this brief life, his spiritual work was to understand his own heritage more deeply. As a teacher of comparative religion once put it, "Sometimes we must go to the stranger to learn to look for the treasures under our own hearthstone."

The Bible, I submit, is full of peculiar treasures for us because it is our culture's most basic religious and spiritual classic. And the very definition of a classic is a work that is not exhausted by a single reading or interpretation, much less the simple and crude understandings we may have had of it as children. Nor even by those we came to in the process of our first critical thinking, since those are often tinged with caricature, anger, or ridicule. No, it bears and merits repeated reinterpretations and fresh understandings.

A good liberal hymn says, "Revelation is not sealed;/ Answ'ring now to our endeavor,/ Truth and right are still revealed."[4] Or as Emerson said, "God speaketh, not spake." We know that religious truth did not appear all in the past. That it did not all get sealed between the covers of the Bible. We are spiritual beneficiaries and descendents of the Renaissance humanists who insisted that the Bible is human literature about the divine, not divine literature about humans, and therefore requires the same critical approach as any other literature. We are the spiritual beneficiaries and descendents of radical reformers who insisted that the scriptures should be available to everyone, so that all might claim their powers of interpretation and understanding.

The chapters that follow are aimed at making it a bit easier for skeptics, seekers, and liberals to do just that. I do not claim that they are more than they are. They are far from being the final words about the Bible. They are probably not even *my* final words on the topic. They constitute only a very basic, thematic introduction to the Bible's varied contents. Though comprehensive in touching on all the canonical Hebrew and Christian scriptures — and some of the non-canonical as well — this is no comprehensive textbook of the sort that would be used in academic study. Though useful, many such books tell the ordinary reader more about history, archeology, the chronology of ancient kings, or the development of textual traditions than one ever really wished to know.

Nor is this a comprehensive treatment of "the Bible as literature." There are some wonderful volumes in that category as well, offering many pleasures. Some have essays on the various books of the Bible by contemporary literary figures. Others are focused more on things like Greek epistolary rhetoric and Paul's style as a writer, or the development and forms of Hebrew poetry. A few even offer dramatic and controversial interpretations of the changing character of the Bible's main protagonist, God.[5]

No, this volume is addressed to skeptics — not to remove your skepticism, but to direct it where it really matters. It is addressed to religious liberals, even radicals, and progressive people of every cause and stripe, to help you claim your own power to understand and to interpret the Bible, both for yourself and for the common good. And it is addressed to seekers of deeper ethical and spiritual wisdom for the everyday living we do together.

I have sometimes used a simple phrase to describe my overarching perspective on life. It's shaped, I say, by a "biblical humanism." In using the term "humanist" I am not refusing to think about God or to search for transcendence. I am identifying with a great tradition of critical thinking about the scriptures, going back to the scholars of the Renaissance and Reformation. They approached the Bible as one would any other human text. What they were interested in was uncovering — revealing — the human experience of the Holy, of God, of enduring truth and wisdom lying behind the veil of the ancient texts.

But I am not interested in using my critical skills only to tear apart or dismiss the religious experience of others in the name of my supposed "scientific" superiority or cultural modernity. That kind of "humanism" partakes of the cultural, pseudo-scientific superiority proclaimed by the Nazis. In his great novel of World War II, *Babi Yar*, Anatoli Kuznetzov remarks about how often they proclaimed that humanism, *German* humanism, was superior to all traditional, "weak" biblical altruism, even as they co-opted many Christians and slaughtered those whom they blamed for that tradition, the Jews.

No, I take the term "biblical humanist" from one of the Nazis early opponents: the German Jewish sage Martin Buber. When the Nazi SS came into the home of this great scholar and professor of comparative religion, he was at work on his new translation of the Hebrew Bible into German — the standard one by Luther having contributed to German anti-Semitism. They demanded that he surrender all his "subversive literature." Buber handed them his Hebrew text of the Bible. "Here," he said, "is the most subversive book in the house."

Indeed it is. In my reading, like his, the biblical tradition challenges every attempt to worship the part in place of the whole. That's its very definition of idolatry. Approached as a humanist, it still challenges the human tendency to idolatries of self, of self-interest, of blood, soil, nation, or race.

The late theologian and social ethicist James Luther Adams taught me most about this. Adams told of spending an evening with the great psychologist Erich Fromm, the author of *The Art of Loving*. Fromm had been saying he wasn't "religious." "Erich," said Adams, "you say you are a 'humanist.' But tell me: what *really* makes you tick?" After a long silence, Fromm replied, "You are right. It's the spirit of the Hebrew prophets in me that gives me my sense of direction. Their cry for justice, their abhorrence of idols, their fidelity to a God who is beyond all image, yet who works and calls us in human history to real equality, community, and personhood. That's what makes me tick."

A humanist need not be one who denies the human need for transcendence or that unimaginable "subversive" God who upsets all our tribal idolatries. One can be biblically grounded and yet find that the authority of the Bible lies not in some supernatural claim to special revelation, but in the human experience of being so subverted and turned toward "real equality, community, and personhood."

So working on understanding the Bible can change you. It does require work, however. The Bible is ancient, complex, and challenging, so it can be a humbling book to explore. That is part of its value.

When I was a child, I understood the Bible quite simply, as a child might. When I began to do critical thinking, I was given to simple challenges or rejections of the Bible, often without much deep understanding of what it was really trying to say when it most disturbed me. When I began to uncover some of its enduring but nonliteral wisdom, its ethical/spiritual wisdom, I felt an urge to share some of what I had begun to find on my journey. The purpose of this book is to make the effort just a bit easier for others. We all need to move from literalism, through simplistic rejection, to an understanding ability to separate the biblical wheat from the chaff. I urge you to use this guide to claim your own power to understand the Bible.

Traditions: Where Does the Bible Come From?

When we ask the question "Where do religious traditions come from?" one answer is obvious. They come from human beings. They arise in time. They are finite. In time, some die. Like humans, they are flawed, particular, and peculiar in character. They fall short of perfection, of their own ideals, and certainly of the glory of God.

Another answer is that, despite all this, they come *from* God. They touch the timeless. They speak of the Infinite. They transcend the generations. They call us to that which is most noble, universal, and generous in our character. Like our children, they somehow seem to come through us, but not from us. They are gifts of God — of the mysterious spirit of life itself.

Some believe that only one of these answers can be true: either/or. A given tradition is either divinely given or humanly made. Others believe that both can be true: both/and. All religious traditions, including our own, are products of human experience and history. But they may also teach us something about the nature of both, by pointing from within to that which transcends us all: the enduring human experience of the "dual mystery of being alive and knowing that we will have to die," as Forrest Church puts it. In this, they partake of the divine, even as human beings do, touching the creative Source of life and death that gave them birth in the first place.

God is said to have created the world itself because God loves stories. And so do we. Perhaps it is because our lives, like all stories, have a beginning, a middle, and an end. But what is the meaning? Underneath so much of our religious, philosophical, historical, scientific seeking lies a persistent, unanswerable question: What kind of story are we in? Is it an unremitting tragedy? A mere farce? A divine (or human) comedy? Or something more complex than any of these genres?

Certainly the Bible, since it is not so much a single book as an entire library, would suggest that our forebears understood that human life can only be meaningfully understood when we see it as a complex story made up of multiple instances of creation, generation, liberation, exultation, frustration, redemption, expectation, inspiration, proclamation, passion, resurrection, incarnation, salvation, and revelation — among other things.

These themes, however, are only broad abstractions — without the stories themselves. We understand what they mean in our own lives only when we encounter them in stories that remind us of something deeply shared in the challenge of human living. Looking at the stories of the Bible not only raises questions about the experiences behind the stories, and about the meanings they have held through the ages for those who passed them on to us, but also challenges us to face some questions ourselves: What does this story mean for me? What challenging questions does it pose about the living of my life? Sometimes I think our resistance to facing such deeper questions may be part of our resistance to trying to understand the Bible at a deeper level.

When looking at a given tradition, however, it is best to separate two sets of questions: First, "Where did this story come from, and what did it mean to those who told it?" And then second, "What does this story now mean for me, for us, who are living today?" This can help us avoid at least some of the temptation to reduce a story to what we want it to mean, without asking ourselves what it meant for those who heard and read the story in its earlier contexts. It can also help us appreciate that even those who first set down the stories in writing, having heard or inherited them, could not avoid adding something of themselves: telling the stories in relation to their own contemporary set of concerns and meanings.

So there are at least two ways to get a Bible story to reveal its truths to you more fully. One is to take the story as story and simply try to enter into it personally, as a character in the drama, taking first one part, then another. Think of one of the stories told by or about Jesus. How does it feel to be the elder brother in the Parable of the Prodigal Son (Luke 15)? Or to be Martha, or her sister Mary, giving him both hospitality and a hearing (Luke 10)? This "transformative" approach to biblical study, especially in small groups, can truly live up to its popular name. I urge you to try it; it offers a way to learn not only about the

Bible, but also about yourself, and about the responses of others to these classic stories.[1]

Another way is less "from the inside out" than "from the outside in." This has do with learning something of "the story of the story." In a sense, that is where we begin here. How did the biblical tradition develop? Where did its stories come from? How do its later stories build on earlier themes and traditions?

To answer such questions fully requires a rather encyclopedic knowledge not only of the texts themselves, but of various contexts in ancient history and literature. As scholars will acknowledge, the story *about* the stories soon becomes far more complex than the stories themselves. But knowing at least some of that larger context seems essential to understanding the stories themselves. Otherwise we will soon be guilty of reading "out of context" and may miss understanding how a given story came to join and fit in with a whole tradition of which it is a part. So the very purpose of this book is to convey, as simply as possible, some of the more illuminating current scholarship about the Bible.

When we ask, "Who wrote the Bible?" we are immediately reminded that the Bible is often called, at least by those who accept its full spiritual authority, "the word of God." Yet its various parts and books are all attributed to named human beings. Nowhere in the Bible is there a claim that God literally wrote or dictated the Bible.[2] The books of the Hebrew and Christian scriptures are attributed to mere human beings, however inspired they may have been.

Many of the attributions of authorship in the Bible, however, are more about *traditions* than about individuals. Take the beginning (and core) of the Hebrew Bible, for example. It's known as the Torah, or the Pentateuch, the "Five Books of Moses." The English names of these books, however, are all derived from a stage in the tradition when the Hebrew text had been translated into Greek: Genesis, Exodus, Leviticus, Numbers, and Deuteronomy.

Only the ultra-orthodox claim the Five Books of Moses were actually written *by* Moses. Especially since they include a narration about the *death* of Moses! Written *by* Moses? They may contain some oral traditions that go back to the time of Moses and the Exodus, at least in a few poems. But they took their present form through a complex evolution.

Here is a summary of how scholars, starting at the beginning of modern biblical studies, began to uncover the interweaving of traditions and stories within these first five books:[3]

Early on they noticed that some stories are repetitions (doublets) of others. Then they noticed that one set of stories habitually refers to God with the sacred Hebrew name, *YHWH*—Yahweh, or Jehovah. The other set uses a form of the more generic term for God in the Semitic languages, *Elohim*—interestingly a feminine plural or collective, equivalent to the Latin *divinitas*, "the divine." They called these strands of tradition, respectively, J and E.

Next they noticed that in some places within the E traditions there were further doublets, and a distinct set of stories and traditions concerned with priestly matters of worship, purity, ritual, and law. They called these traditions by the letter P. Finally, they saw that the Book of Deuteronomy, like those that immediately followed it, were written in a distinctive style and shared a similar theology, in which God acts in history to reward just and faithful rulers and to bring down the unfaithful. They called this tradition D.

Before we go further with this story, however, some chronology is probably in order. Leave aside for the moment the primordial stories of creation itself and of legendary time, from Adam and Eve through Noah and his descendents. These now introduce the Pentateuch, but as we shall see, they are not necessarily the oldest materials it contains.

Next come the stories of Abraham and his wife, Sarah, leaving the city of Ur in ancient Mesopotamia (modern Iraq) and traveling around the so-called "Fertile Crescent" to the hill country beyond the Jordan, then down to Egypt and back. Migrations like this, archeology and inscriptions confirm, are consistent with the developments starting around 1900 B.C.E. (Before the Common Era), in the Middle Bronze Age. The largely legendary, patriarchal stories of Abraham, Isaac, and Jacob (later renamed Israel) would fall in the century or centuries following. Then come the stories of the children of Israel, starting with Joseph, going down into Egypt, and becoming enslaved there. These try to portray events that would have to have happened between 1800 and 1200 B.C.E.

The real heart of the Hebrew national epic, however, is the story of Moses and of the Israelites being liberated from Egyptian slavery.

Whether the Hebrews can be identified with foreign workers called "Hapiru" in Egyptian inscriptions is a matter of some debate. Moses, however, is an Egyptian name, and a departure of bonded laborers from Egypt to Canaan is consistent with historical conditions circa 1200 B.C.E., though scholars continue to debate just which pharaoh was involved.[4]

The next two centuries are the era depicted in the books of Joshua and Judges, before the tribes of Israel became as other nations, united under a monarchy. Samuel is the prophet who anoints first Saul as king, then David; the second part of the narrative associated with Samuel narrates the "court history" of King David, in all of its soap-opera drama. The reign of David's son by Bathsheba, Solomon, after the year 1000 B.C.E., marked the Golden Age of Israel, when its first temple was built in Jerusalem.

Soon after Solomon died, around 922 B.C.E., his empire was divided into two kingdoms: Judah in the south, with its capital at Jerusalem, and Israel in the north, with its capital at Shechem. Prophets arise to warn kings and priests of both realms against departing from God's ways, but to no avail. The Assyrians conquered and ended the northern kingdom of Israel in 722 B.C.E. Jerusalem and Judah fell to the Babylonians in 587, and the last king of Judah was carried off to exile. And there endeth the Book of Kings. The exile lasted for nearly fifty years. Then Cyrus of Persia defeats the Babylonians and, in 539, he allowed the Jews to return. Nehemiah, serving as the Persian governor of Judah, was allowed to rebuild the walls of Jerusalem, and the priest, Ezra, to conduct Yahwist worship in a rebuilt, smaller second temple.

The various strands of the biblical tradition seem to come into existence at key moments in this larger national story. The J traditions, for example, seem clearly concerned with Judah and may have been first collected and written in the era of Solomon, in the 900s.[5] Meanwhile the E traditions develop in the north, perhaps around the sanctuary of Shiloh.[6]

Both traditions combine stories of Moses and the Exodus with stories of the patriarchs, Abraham, Isaac, and Jacob. But the J tradition emphasizes the originality and importance of God's covenant with Abraham. The E tradition says more about the importance of the Exodus and the covenant at Mt. Sinai. While recounting how God's proper name, YHWH, is first revealed to Moses, it generally uses the more generic term for God, connected to the high god in the Canaanite pantheon, El.

It is as though the two strands of tradition develop with different emphases. Then they are recombined—probably after the fall of the northern kingdom, when many of its survivors combined forces with the kingdom of Judah in the south. This reweaving of J and E would then have taken place after 722 B.C.E. Then, during the reign of King Josiah of Judah, in the year 622, as we are told in 2 Kings 22, a "book of the law" was discovered in the Temple at Jerusalem. It commanded a reform of worship, concentrating it all in one central shrine. This "book of the law" was the core of D, the Deuteronomic tradition. An editor in that tradition soon assembled that book as both a set of final speeches given by Moses before dying and as the first book in a continuous "sacred history"—comprising Deuteronomy, Joshua, Judges, Samuel, and Kings, down to Josiah.[7]

When exile came thirty-five years later, the last few kings were added.

What we know as the Pentateuch, however, starting with the creation story in Genesis, did not come together in anything resembling its present form until the crisis of the Exile, and perhaps not until the time of Nehemiah and Ezra, around 450 B.C.E. The P traditions, with their concerns for law, ritual, and worship, emerge from the crisis of the destruction of Solomon's Temple and the need to preserve its traditions—or from the need to reassemble those traditions for the new temple in the Second Commonwealth. Certainly the Torah served as something of a "constitution" for the new state led by the priest Ezra and the governor, Nehemiah. In Nehemiah 8, Ezra reads it out loud to all the people.

It is also around this time that the Hebrew Bible acquires its traditional three divisions. In Hebrew, those divisions are called Torah (the Pentateuch), Nevi'im (the Prophets), and Ketuvim (the Writings). In Judaism, these give the Hebrew scriptures the name Tanakh, from the first letters of the three divisions—T, N, and K.

Torah consists of the five books of Moses we have been discussing. Nevi'im, the Prophets, has eight scrolls or books: the four scrolls of so-called "Former Prophets," which we would call the books of the Deuteronomic history, from Joshua and Judges through Samuel and Kings. (The latter get divided as 1 and 2 Samuel, 1 and 2 Kings in Christian Bibles; in the Tanakh they are counted as single scrolls.)

Then come the four scrolls of "Latter Prophets"—Isaiah, Jeremiah, Ezekiel, and "the Twelve"—the last made up of the twelve so-called "minor prophets," from Hosea through Malachi—in Christian Bibles, twelve separate books.

As these traditions developed, later materials were often included as part of earlier materials with which they had an affinity or traditional identification. The first prophet Isaiah, for example, whose work began "in the year that King Uzziah died" (742 B.C.E.), has his scroll added to by the prophecies of a Second Isaiah, clearly speaking just before the end of the Exile (ca. 539 B.C.E.), and perhaps of a Third Isaiah, who wrote still later (ca. 530–510 B.C.E.). No distinction appears in the Bible. They are all just "Isaiah." This process of attribution is a far cry from our modern notion of authorship, but it is persistent in the process of biblical tradition formation.

The third great division of the Bible, the Ketuvim, or Writings, is a miscellany containing numerous examples of such attribution. The Psalms, for example, are attributed to David, though some clearly date from five hundred years after his death, during the Exile. The Proverbs are similarly attributed to Solomon the Wise, but most have a much later origin. The Writings also include the story of Job, the five scrolls later liturgically associated with the major Jewish holidays (Song of Songs, Ruth, Lamentations, Ecclesiastes, and Esther), the late prophet Daniel, and the histories of Ezra, Nehemiah, and Chronicles. Traditionally, the canon (normative list) of the Tanakh consists of only these twenty-four books.

Sacred writings continued to be produced, however. The Persian period ended around 330 B.C.E. with the conquests of Alexander the Great and his successors. Greek began to displace local languages in the Eastern Mediterranean, especially for writing. By the time of the Maccabean Revolt in 166–160 B.C.E., even Jews in Palestine no longer spoke Hebrew, but rather Aramaic. The international written language, especially for Jews outside Palestine, in the diaspora, was Greek. The largest such Jewish community, at Alexandria in Egypt, commissioned a Greek translation of the Hebrew scriptures. It was called the Septuagint, after the seventy scholars said to have done the translation. As non-Jews (Gentiles) were attracted to Jewish monotheism, it was this Greek text that they knew as "ta Biblia" (literally, "the books").

Jewish sacred writings continued to appear, but now often in Greek. Which could be considered to be inspired? Those with original texts in Hebrew had an advantage, especially among Jews resistant to assimilation. This was even more true after 70 C.E. In the wake of the destruction of Jerusalem and the Temple by the Romans, the rabbis knew that only a common scripture could hold together the people of God. They began to establish a canon, or norm, for a Hebrew text of the Bible.

In many synagogues, however, the Septuagint continued to be used. Jews like Paul and Gentiles like Timothy who accepted Jesus as the messiah both used it as their Bible. Meanwhile they and other early Christians were generating writings of their own that were read at church gatherings. Yet there was no broad agreement about which of these newer writings merited universal use in Christian worship until a crisis of church unity showed the need for one.

In the middle of the second century, a wealthy Gentile-Christian named Marcion proposed a form of Christian faith that radically rejected its Jewish roots. Marcionite Christianity wished to cease identifying the God of Jesus with the God of the Hebrew Bible, to cease using the Hebrew scriptures at all, and to define its scripture as consisting only of the letters of Paul and a gospel edited from the one by his Gentile follower, Luke. Since Jesus had so clearly worshiped the God of Israel, the Christian bishops rejected Marcion's ideas. They decided that catholic (universal) Christians would continue to use the Hebrew Bible (in its Septuagint translation). Beyond that, the Christian bishops had to decide, just as the rabbis had, which writings would constitute the canonical scriptures of their community and of its new covenant (Latin, *testamentum*) in Christ. They accepted the letters of Paul and certain others that claimed his authority or that of other apostles. They included not just Luke's version of the gospel, but four gospels that claimed authority from apostles who had known Jesus in the flesh.

They gave first place to one attributed to Matthew, which presented Jesus clearly within the Hebrew tradition, as the fulfillment of all its prophecies.

When it came to including Christian prophecy, however, they were more ambivalent. Just as there had been some rabbis who were uncertain about whether the apocalyptic visions of the prophet Daniel should be included (as they finally were), so among Christians the last book included was Revelation — a set of apocalyptic visions attributed to the apostle John. As late as the fourth century C.E. there were still some Christians, thinking it too idiosyncratic and easily misinterpreted, who wanted to leave the book of Revelation out of the Bible.

In this process of sorting through the traditions to establish the normative contents for the Hebrew Bible and the Christian scriptures, many other writings certainly *were* left out. The final rabbinic, or Masoretic, text of the Hebrew Bible, for example, did not include even all of the writings that had been included in the Septuagint translation. Additions to Jewish sacred writings had continued to be produced in Greek. As mainstream Christianity decided to continue use of the Septuagint, it accepted some of these writings. When St. Jerome translated the Bible into Latin (the "Vulgate"), he set apart those texts that were outside the Hebrew canon.

These so-called "apocrypha" include interesting works like First and Second Maccabees, with the story of Hannukah; the so-called Wisdom of Solomon; and Ecclesiasticus, or the Wisdom of Jesus, son of Sirach, and almost a dozen others. They have a place in Catholic and Eastern Orthodox Bibles as "deutero-canonical" books, but not in most Protestant ones. Anglican Bibles print them, but in a separate section, between what Christians call the Old Testament and the New Testament.

You will notice that I avoid both those terms. They tend to imply a Christian attitude that the latter has somehow superseded the former — a none-too-subtle form of anti-Judaism. Since World War II, and since the Second Vatican Council, many Christians have begun to be more careful and honest about the Christian heritage of anti-Judaism and anti-Semitism. Along with many others today, I prefer to speak of the Hebrew Bible and the Christian scriptures, recognizing that for Christians the full Bible includes the former.

The canonical New Testament, however, also deliberately left out many other writings produced as scripture by early Christians. Just how many we will perhaps never know. When Christianity became the official religion of the Roman empire, after Constantine and the Council of Nicea (325 C.E.), many of these noncanonical writings were destroyed as promoting one form or another of heresy—often a form of so-called gnosticism.

Gnosticism, historically, was a part of Hellenistic culture that stretched well beyond the biblical traditions. It emphasized spiritual knowledge (Greek *gnosis*) or wisdom. At its extremes, Gnosticism could be (and still can be, because it is still popular) rather esoteric and even foolish, speculating about the ethereal in other worlds, rather than attending to the weightier issues of compassion and justice in this one. Still another tendency in Gnosticism is toward a dualism of spirit and matter, rejecting the body and the created world in favor of the process of transcending these through special spiritual knowledge or understanding. Gnosticism can attempt to embody wisdom, but it can also be elitist, with special spiritual knowledge being transferred as a kind of "spiritual commodity" from elite spiritual master to chosen disciple, often to the detriment of the equal worth and dignity of everyone in the commonwealth of God. Rather like much "New Age" spirituality today.

In recent years some of the scriptures of Gnostic Christians have come to light. An entire library of ancient Gnostic manuscripts was found in 1948 at Nag Hammadi in Egypt, and has now been fully published, for example. Feminist scholars have been particularly interested. Not only are the epistles, gospels, and other writings of Gnostic Christians attributed to disciples like Thomas and Philip, but also to women disciples like Mary Magdalene. It has also become clear that the Gnostic approach to Christianity allowed some early Christian women to claim direct inspiration from God or Christ, without going through the bishops, presbyters, and other male authorities.

Moreover, *gnosis* had affinities with an understanding of God's eternal Wisdom as feminine (*Hokmah*, feminine, in Hebrew; *Sophia* in Greek). There are vestiges of this even within what feminists call the "malestream" and canonical tradition. Some feminists therefore recommend transgressing the boundaries of that tradition in order to re-claim a more accurate as well as inclusive picture of early Christian inspiration and wisdom.[8]

This summary of tradition formation makes one thing clear: today not all people who use the Bible, either for worship or for study, use exactly the same Bible. Which brings us to the question of versions: Which Bible should *I* use?

Versions: Which Bible Should I Read?

When fundamentalists propose posting the Ten Commandments in public buildings, the ACLU lawyer in me always wants to ask, "Which version? Protestant, Catholic, or Jewish?" Although most people in our so-called Judeo-Christian culture assume the texts are the same, in fact they vary somewhat.[1]

Likewise when people in our culture speak of "the Bible," they overlook the differences between Jewish, Catholic, and Protestant versions—and usually mean the last. We have already seen how the rabbinic text of the Hebrew scriptures consists only of the Tanakh's twenty-four books of Torah, Nevi'im, and Ketuvim. Early Christians used an expanded version of those scriptures translated into Greek and known as the Septuagint. When Christianity had become the official religion of the Roman Empire, a translation for use in the Latin West was prepared by Jerome and became known as the Vulgate. Yet unless one has the ability to read Hebrew, Greek, or Latin, all this is just background. The real questions are these: Which version of the Bible should I use? In which English translation?

During the Middle Ages, translating the Latin Bible into the language of ordinary people was forbidden. It challenged the authority of the priestly caste to read and interpret the sacred texts. Knowledge of Hebrew and Greek was largely lost even in scholarly circles until the Renaissance. When the Protestant Reformation came in the sixteenth century, the reformers wanted not only to make the Bible available to ordinary readers for study but also sought to emulate Jerome in translating the "Old Testament" directly from the Hebrew. In so doing, they chose to omit texts that the Septuagint and Vulgate had taken not from Hebrew but from later Greek additions to the Hebrew scriptures.

Christians also changed the traditional structure of the Hebrew Bible. They distributed the Writings, the Ketuvim, in a quasi-chronological fashion among the Prophets, ending with the latter. In this way, the "Old Testament" ended, not with a recapitulation of the sacred history of the Jews in the Book of Chronicles, but with the late prophet Malachi. This made the whole Hebrew Bible seem as though it culminated in prophecies that could be taken as referring to the coming of Jesus — even though their meaning in the original Hebrew context had been quite different. They also divided longer texts like Samuel, Kings, Chronicles, and Ezra/Nehemiah into two books each and counted the Twelve so-called "minor prophets" not as a single scroll, but each as a separate book. So where the Tanakh had only twenty-four books, Protestant versions of the Hebrew Bible counted thirty-nine books, while Catholic versions had forty-six.

So choosing a Bible has not just to do with which *version* you may want, but also with which *translation*— a process that has been with us for millennia. It always has its problems.

Every translation is liable to introduce word choices that begin as a simple mistake and end as a theological interpretation. One classic example dates back to the Septuagint. When the Christian evangelist Matthew quotes the prophet Isaiah, he uses the Septuagint, having Isaiah say, "Behold, a virgin shall conceive and bear a son." The Greek word in question, *parthenos,* does refer to a woman's sexual status. But the word used by Isaiah in the original Hebrew had no such meaning. It merely meant "young woman." So translation influenced the theological idea of virgin birth.

The first authorized translation of the Bible into English also introduced what have become some "beloved mistranslations." The King James Version of 1611 influenced the very shape of the English language, just as Martin Luther's translation of the Bible helped to give shape to German. This is the translation used in older family Bibles and in the Gideon Bibles found in hotel room drawers all across America. Its rhythms and diction are those we continue to regard as familiar, traditional, and, well, "biblical."

In Psalm 96, for example, the KJV uses a beautiful phrase when it speaks of worshiping the Lord "in the beauty of holiness." It doesn't thrill me a bit to learn that modern scholars now believe that the proper translation for the obscure Hebrew behind those words may have more to do with wearing attractive priestly garments than it does with holiness of character. I would almost rather keep the error. One edition of the King James Version, the so-called "Wicked Bible" of 1631, included a typographical mistake in the Ten Commandments, omitting the word 'not' to say, "Thou shalt commit adultery." Don't look for it in the Gideon edition, however; the error has been corrected.

Beloved and traditional as the King James Version may be, it has other disadvantages for our purposes today. Not only is it rather heavy on the "th" sound, as thou speakest not and understandeth not readily, but its sentence structure and archaic vocabulary can be downright puzzling. So more modern translations have been developed. Many.

One popular among more evangelical Christians is the New International Version (NIV). Perhaps the most widely used, however, is still the Revised Standard Version (RSV), which was done under the sponsorship of the National Council of Churches in the USA after World War II. It attempts to update the KJV by removing the archaisms and correcting the mistranslations, though without losing the familiar rhythms in familiar places. After concern for gender-inclusive language became important, a New Revised Standard Version (NRSV) was issued.

Some editions of these translations also include the Apocrypha, the deutero-canonical books included in Catholic Bibles but not traditional Protestant ones. This is true also of the New English Bible (NEB)—a totally new, fresh translation in contemporary British English, of considerable literary quality and easy to read. In familiar passages, however, the NEB lacks the KJV rhythms that the RSV tries to preserve, and it tends to translate even some terms that are neuter in Greek with masculine pronouns in English. The more recent Revised English Bible (REB) is more gender-inclusive.

Just how far to go with gender-inclusive language is a controversial topic, however, even among feminist scholars. After all, the Bible, like nearly everything else ancient, is the product of a patriarchal culture. How far do you go in changing sexist terms before a translation becomes not a translation but a tendentious paraphrase?

Paraphrase goes rather beyond translation. Some paraphrase editions are quite popular. But their tendentiousness is generally anything but feminist. Their sponsorship is usually conservative and evangelical, not ecumenical, and their aim is to make the Bible (especially the New Testament) readily accessible and simplified. And that's the trouble. They gloss over difficulties. And when they do, it is often in order to make traditional orthodox piety shine through more simply and clearly. The evangelical motives may be understandable. But I can't recommend the results for study purposes. Paraphrase editions include *The Living Bible, The Good News Bible,* and *Good News for Modern Man,* among others.

There are also translations with a "slant," however, that can offer new insights into ideas or passages that have become commonplace. You can see what I mean by reading Paul's hymn to love in 1 Corinthians 13 in the remarkable English translation by J. B. Phillips. Clarence Jordan, the founder of the interracial Koinonia Community in south Georgia, did a "rendering" of the New Testament into the Southern vernacular. Jordan called it *The Cottonpatch Version of the Gospel.* In it, Jerusalem becomes Atlanta, the scribes and Pharisees are the deacons of the Baptist and Methodist churches, and Jesus tells his disciples not "Be ye perfect..." but "Be mature..." That last translation is quite accurate, too. The Greek word means "inclusive, complete." "So be mature, taking everyone into account, just as your Father in heaven does."

It can also be fun to look at how translations into other languages bring new insights. Read a French New Testament, for example, and you'll find that "Blessed are the meek" in French is "*Heureuxs sont les debonairs.*" Literally, "Happy are the debonair."

The Douay Version of the Bible is the Catholic translation done in that city in France to compete with the Protestant King James Bible. Later updates were often called *Confraternity.* The most recent Catholic translation is called the New American Bible (NAB), while the Jerusalem Bible (JB) often provides some strikingly fresh alternative language. The best English translation of the Hebrew Bible, the Tanakh, came from the Jewish Publication Society in 1985. It does not, of course, include the Christian scriptures however.

If you already have a Tanakh, or wish to acquire one, you can certainly use it with the first section of this book. If you already have a standard modern Christian Bible in English (NIV, RSV, NRSV, NEB, or REB; NAB, Jerusalem, Catholic, or Confraternity), any one of these will do well enough. Beware, however, of paraphrase editions that are not scholarly translations. Beware also of trying to use the KJV, especially in annotated editions, since these often have theological assumptions that are quite biased. If, on the other hand, you are going to go out and buy a new Bible, you might do well to consider buying a study edition. The notes will be there to supplement what you will read here. Among these, I would recommend one of the following:

New Oxford Annotated Bible with the Apocrypha (NRSV)
Oxford Study Bible (REB)
Catholic Study Bible (NAB)

Unless otherwise noted, I will use the New Revised Standard Version text and translation.

Interpretations: Reading the Bible to Challenge Oppression

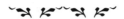

All understandings of the Bible are interpretations. There is no one, final meaning for all people in all times and places. Part of the purpose of this book is to help you claim your own ability to understand and interpret these traditions. But some interpretations are better informed than others. Some are more useful, edifying, inspirational, or enduring. Some are clearly oppressive and some are empowering. The same can be said of understandings of God. Some are far more mature than others.

It is easy to have a bad experience with the Bible. Authority figures may have offered an interpretation that seems, and is, unjust and oppressive. Those who sit down to read the Bible entirely on their own, however, can have an equally bad experience. Trying to read the Bible through from beginning to end, many people get bogged down somewhere in the patriarchal list of "begats" or in the long historical books, bored and alienated.

Skeptics, seekers, and religious liberals are also likely to bring to their reading questions that easily bring forth negative answers. While these questions are important, they can also set up barriers to a deeper understanding of what is really going on in the Bible. The first set of questions is historical: Did this really happen this way? The second set of questions is both personal and theological: How do I feel about God in this story? Isolating those questions from one another will not help. They are inevitably related.

It is very easy to say "This didn't happen!" As they sing in *Porgy and Bess,* "It ain't necessarily so!" In a given story, that may be quite true. One does not have to take the Bible literally when it says Methuselah lived nine hundred years. That is clearly the stuff of legend. It is also easy to say, "This God is oppressive!" We know how some images of God have been used to try to justify violence and injustice. What we easily forget is how a given legend may both reflect and try to transcend the realities of ancient society.

For the Bible, God and history are intertwined. Human history in all cultures is full of oppression, violence, and cruelty. So it is not surprising that the Bible should have mixed images of God's role in history. There are two remarkable things, however, about the Bible's treatment of history and of God. One concerns its honesty about history. Rather than tell only the good side of Israel's story, the Hebrew Bible often tries to take a God's-eye view of things and tell the bad as well. The other remarkable thing is that God is most often seen to be on the side of the poor and the oppressed, to be seeking the abasement of the oppressors and the empowerment of those who are being denied their freedom and human dignity. In the Christian scriptures, this means extending hope beyond the tragedies of history and bringing new life out of death itself.

A student was once asked by his rabbi, "Who is the most tragic character in the Bible?" "It's not Job," the student ventured. "Not Jacob or Saul . . . Hm." "Not bad for a beginner," said the rabbi. "The most tragic figure is God, who suffers with every bad thing that happens."

Not everything in the Bible actually did happen, of course, or happen in the way it is described. Granted. But a remarkable amount of the biblical story does find at least some extra-biblical confirmation. The core of the "sacred story" does deal with actual history.

That history is prefaced by legends from prehistory going back before human memory to the beginning of time, followed by stories of the legendary forebears who link the Israelites to their neighbors. But the heart of the sacred story is Israel's liberation from bondage in Egypt. Obviously there are elements of myth and legend there, too, as in all epic stories. It doesn't end gloriously, however. The epic goes on to recount the rise and fall of Israel down to the end of the line of Davidic kings in 2 Kings 25.

Then the next book, Chronicles, begins to repeat the whole story again in abbreviated form, starting with a list of "begats": "Adam, Seth, Enoch . . . ," etc. Obviously, the further back the compilers of this history went, the more they had to rely not simply on oral traditions, but on the more mythic, legendary parts of those traditions. For the material going back to the time of King David and his son, Solomon, they had more documentary evidence: early court histories, it would seem. The sacred story becomes more historical as it goes along.

Something similar can be said of God. Throughout the story the normative image of God (though God is also supposed to be beyond all earthly image) is derived from the core of the national epic. It is an image of God as both creator and liberator. Yet because there are different strands of tradition woven together in the Bible, from different eras of religious development, perhaps we should not be surprised if some early images of God are not all that exalted. They are, in fact, images of a very tribal, patriarchal, and nationalistic God, not a more universal God who, as creator and liberator, ultimately also judges the deeds of all the nations in history.

It is a great temptation for us to sit in judgment on the Judge, as it were: to read the Bible as though it were a modern novel, asking ourselves whether we like the protagonist (God) or not. Probably not; not according to our contemporary ideals and standards at least. Whether this is fair of us or not, however, is an understandable historical question worth our asking. After all, we are dealing with a story that is thousands of years old. If God is just a character in the story, then perhaps we should at least notice this about God in the Bible: God gets better. Seemingly arbitrary, unforgiving, judgmental, and even cruel at first, God grows up and mellows. Perhaps as we read, so should we.

Jack Miles makes this point in his remarkable book *God: A Biography*. There may be limitations to his method of trying to read the Bible the way we would a novel, however, and God as the leading character in the story. This is especially true when we come to the Christian scriptures. When Miles takes them up in his more recent book, *Christ: A Crisis in the Life of God,* his own premises require him to treat Jesus less as a human figure in history with a divine mission than as God-in-the-flesh. This forces him to see the crucifixion as nothing less than a self-destructive, suicidal crisis in the life of God! This favors only one tradition about Jesus, derived from the Gospel of John, over other interpretations from the other three canonical gospels. It also sets aside, for the sake of a literary approach, all efforts to understand Jesus as a more historical and human figure. It also ends, finally, with an odd reversal of traditional theology, in which Jesus is seen as entirely God while God is seen as all too human.

Some interpretations of the Bible, then, are almost entirely literary. Others are almost entirely historical. The approach taken here will try to balance the two. As we have seen, the sacred story may have a historical core. But it is not simply history. If we approach it that way, we will end up prejudging too many of its stories negatively. Rather when faced with legends and miracle stories, we would do better to ask, "What was the purpose of this story? What deeper insights was it intended to convey?"

After all, human experiences within history demand metaphors that transcend that history in order to interpret what we have experienced. In the biblical tradition, God is, at the very least, the ultimate such metaphor. We may be complete agnostics about God and skeptics about the actual historicity of events like the exodus from Egypt or the resurrection of Jesus. These, too, may partake of metaphor. But to understand the Bible requires that we try to understand, at the very least, what it is in human experience that brought forth such transcendent metaphors as creation, liberation, and resurrection.

In other words, you don't need to believe in the God of the Bible to understand its stories. You don't even need to believe that the Bible is consistent in its image of God; it isn't. Neither are we human beings. At times, the Bible's images of God seem tragic, oppressive, punitive, cruel, or destructive. So are we. We violate our covenants with one another and with God, who both judges our failings and constantly offers what the Hebrew Bible calls *hesed*— steadfast, enduring love. Ultimately, we finite human beings are forced to try to understand "God" as best we are able — either as the transcendent reality within the history we live or as ultimate metaphor. The Bible can help either way. All it requires is that we recognize that those who created and repeated its sacred stories had only their experience of history and only metaphors available with which to understand their own experience and that of their forebears.

Even if the Bible remains for us only great literature, and not sacred scripture, we should try to approach it on its own terms: as literature trying to tell us of human experience from a transcendent, God's-eye perspective, trying to remind human beings who had experienced both undeserved goodness and unmerited evil how to remain true to the transcendent source of creation, liberation, and ultimate justice.

Without such an understanding, it is easy to fall into a form of reverse fundamentalism about the Bible. Remember: "The letter kills, but the spirit gives life." Rather than focus on particular proof-texts, moralistic judgments, or overly literal readings, a look at any part of the scriptural tradition should be done in the light of the spirit of the whole. And surely there is good warrant for this. In the Hebrew Bible the prophets warn against idolatry—the worship of the part in place of the whole, of the created thing in place of the Creator. They urge a focus on a larger spirit of covenantal justice, mercy, and humility, not on particular forms of purity or piety. In the Christian scriptures, the core spirit of Jesus' own teachings, especially in the Sermon on the Mount and in the parables, has often been seen as central to interpreting other traditions.

This mode of interpretation is sometimes criticized as preferring "a canon within the canon." All interpretations, however, ultimately give more weight to some traditions than to others. The argument then is over which better reflects the spirit of the whole.

Take issues of sexuality in the Bible. Far from being "sex negative," the overall spirit of the Bible celebrates the body, like Creation, as good. It says faith, hope, and love abide, but the greatest is love. So we need to be careful to ask questions about particular texts that also capture their overall spirit. The story of Sodom, for example, is not about same-sex love; it is about violating basic civility by allowing guests to be raped! Similarly, adultery seen as a spiritual violation of the covenant of marriage; sexual acting out in fertility rites and pagan temple prostitution are seen more as spiritually empty than anything else. Even when we encounter a prohibition like the one in the purity code of Priestly tradition, against "lying with a man as with a woman," we may still want to ask a few historical/interpretative questions before assuming we understand the inner spirit of what is intended. A feminist might ask, for example, "What if the male treated the other male not the way patriarchal society treated women, but as an equal? Is that forbidden, too?" Paul may condemn people leaving the church and giving themselves up to sexual license, but what about faithful loyalty between same-sex partners? Does that fit what he says about how it is better to marry than burn with frustration? And if Christians are to be free from other aspects of the Torah purity codes, like food restrictions and circumcision, why would he want this taboo alone to continue?

It matters, then, what kind of interpretative questions we ask. Too often skeptics, seekers, and liberals confine themselves to the narrow questions with which we began and stay overly literalistic in their interpretations. Some of my own Unitarian forebears, for example, disavowed the doctrine of the Trinity because it does not literally appear in the text of the Bible, but is a matter of later interpretation. Rejection of the miracle stories in the gospels led a liberal like Thomas Jefferson to put together an edition of the New Testament in which none of them appear, calling it "The Life and Morals of Jesus of Nazareth." In flatly dismissing the miracle stories, Jefferson failed to offer an interpretation of what they may have meant to those who first understood Jesus in relation to such stories.

If literalism is one danger, the opposite extreme can be the tendency to treat everything as a symbol of some higher truth or more universal human experience. There is a good cautionary tale in the person of the early Christian theologian Origen of Alexandria (182–251 C.E.). Early in his career, Origen was, if anything, too much of a literalist. When, like Jesus, he allowed women as well as men to study with him, he was slandered as using his female disciples for sex. Reading Matthew 19:12, about "those who have made themselves eunuchs for the sake of the kingdom of heaven," he evidently decided to take the verse literally! Later, however, having repented of his self-mutilation, it is not surprising that he became famous for probing for the deeper, hidden spiritual truths within the texts, using allegorical interpretation. Eventually this, too, got him in trouble. He began to presuppose a division not unlike the one seen by the Gnostic heretics he tried to counter: a division between the vast majority of simple Christians, accepting the church's teaching on faith and motivated by fear, and a minority of more spiritual Christians, who rationally understand their faith and are motivated by love.[1] Origen was ultimately condemned as a heretic.

There *are* symbols in the Bible. But not everything is a mystery that requires a literary analysis. Or as Freud himself reportedly said, "Sometimes a cigar is just a cigar!" One challenge for interpretation is to take *metaphors* for what they are and not to try to read things into them or take them in some "literal" way that ignores their historical context. Many of the worst forms of biblical interpretation, after all, have been attempts to take texts that are replete with symbolic language—apocalyptic imagery in Daniel or Revelations—and read into them aspects of contemporary history. Conservative Christian writers have made a fortune exploiting the anxieties of good people by publishing books with strained, speculative, and despairing interpretations of these texts. One of the all-time best-sellers in this genre is *The Late, Great Planet Earth*, by Hal Lindsey. I have always appreciated the one-sentence review of it once offered by Martin Marty: "This author gave up on the world before God did."

Sound historical-critical interpretation can help show what the symbols used by a given biblical author would have meant within the context of events in their own time, so that we can keep those meanings primary. This, after all, is essential to literary interpretation as well: What type of text are we dealing with here? What were its rhetorical purposes? Right at the beginning of Genesis, for example, we encounter a hymn to the creation and to the Creator, in six stanzas. What sense does it make to debate it as if it were some sort of scientific treatise? A late Christian text such as 1 Peter may seem to reenforce every form of unjust social subordination, telling slaves to be obedient to their masters, women to their husbands, and Christians to their emperor. But a rhetorical analysis of the letter itself in its historical context may reveal an anxious male leadership telling early Christians not to practice egalitarianism or challenge the state. Which, along with other evidence, shows that many were inclined to do so. Saying "Jesus is Lord," for them meant "Caesar is *not* our master." When they said that in Christ there is neither Jew nor Gentile, slave nor free, male nor female, they were offering a discipleship of equals that was radically different from the social hierarchies of the society around them.

Feminist biblical interpretation calls this "reading against the grain." It also insists that when the Bible seems to leave out the voice and agency of women, we should use at first an interpretative strategy of *suspicion*—because surely women were present in the story all along, though marginalized in the process of tradition-formation—and then a strategy of *reconstruction* of their place in the tradition. We will do some of that in this book, with a view toward reading the Bible to overcome oppression and to empower those who have been marginalized both within its traditions and from interpreting its texts to claim their own interpretive power.

During the course of this introduction I will introduce a variety of interpretative approaches—literary, historical, political, feminist. My purpose is not to form some definitive, overall interpretative stance toward the Bible, but to help skeptical, liberal seekers find an entrée to the texts. The interpretations offered here are not definitive because I question whether there is (or should be) any such thing, but neither should my interpretations be mistaken as anti-Christian or anti-Jewish. Biblical interpretation has played too great a role in the history of anti-Semitism for us ever to forget. Sometimes even Christian feminists have found themselves unconsciously contributing to anti-Jewish attitudes by portraying Jesus or the early Christian movement as more enlightened in relation to women's issues than other strains in first-century Judaism. There is simply no reason for such an assumption.

There were, and are, both anti-oppressive and oppressive strains in *all* religious traditions, at all stages of development. Within movements that challenge the status quo, however, as did both the Jesus movement and the strains with Judaism (including the Pharisees) that led to the rabbinic tradition, the voice of women and of others who challenge oppression are more evident. There is a strong and growing revival of Jewish feminist interpretation as well.

Recent developments in Christian biblical scholarship, in fact, are beginning to realize that what is at stake in the differing interpretations of scripture offered by the rabbinic and ecclesiastical traditions are, in fact, two contrasting approaches to *midrash*. *Midrashim* (the plural) are interpretations or investigations of one biblical text in relation to another text or story. Sometimes imaginative stories are created in *midrashim* to reinterpret or make sense of a tradition in light of new understandings or realities.

After the destruction of the Temple in Jerusalem in 70 C.E., for example, the rabbis had to reinterpret the meaning of a great many traditional injunctions and stories. Eventually the rabbis formed a coherent set of reinterpretations and commentary known as the Talmud.

But one way to look at the letters of Paul and the gospels of early Christianity is as an alternative set of *midrashim*, reinterpreting the basic themes of the Hebrew Bible in light of the assertion that the long-awaited messiah has come, in Jesus, and will come again to bring redemption.

Since the rabbis took the text of the Bible to be a seamless whole, *midrashim* often developed to try to explain anomalies where one layer of tradition seemed to contradict another. In Genesis 1, for example, human beings are created in God's image, male and female. In Genesis 2, however, only Adam has been created, and Eve is created from him. Some concluded that two different women were created: the First Woman with Adam, then Eve from him as his wife. Still others identified the First Woman with a mysterious "Lilith" mentioned in Isaiah 34:14, who dwells in a desolate no-man's land, rather like the first woman to give Abraham a child, the Egyptian slave woman Hagar. Since she is the mother of Ishmael, and matriarch of the Arabs, it is not surprising that the Qu'ran gives a reading of her story that is rather different from the one we find in Genesis.

Likewise Paul, though a Jewish contemporary of the first rabbis, offers an interpretation of the Bible that centers more on the story of Abraham and Isaac than on the Exodus and the divine gift of the Torah at Sinai. In fact, for Paul the Law is less a gift than the moment that gives specific legal definition to all the human wrongdoing going back to Adam. So for him the most important characters in the Hebrew Bible are not Moses and Aaron. Instead, they are Adam and Abraham. Because of Adam, what is needed is faith like Abraham's, but in a new "Adam" who is as sinless as the first "son of God" was sinful. This is an entirely different midrashic or allegorical framework.

Some people will argue that the Bible should not be interpreted in anything other than traditional ways. "Which tradition?" of course, is one question. All traditions are themselves interpretations. Another is why anyone should feel compelled to leave the Bible so firmly in the hands of those who would use it to maintain structures of oppression. I say it must be read to liberate — to liberate people, and to liberate the wisdom within the scriptures themselves. As an early New England covenant of faith phrased it, "for God hath yet more light to pour forth from His Holy Word."

The Bible is not threatened by such interpretations. Quite the contrary. During the mid-nineteenth century, the great American minister Theodore Parker (from whom Lincoln took the phrase, "government of the people, by the people, and for the people") was an American pioneer in historical-critical scholarship and progressive biblical interpretation. He was also a strong advocate for the abolition of slavery and for the establishment of women's equality, when many interpreted the Bible as supporting the oppressive status quo. Though one might wish his language were more gender inclusive, listen to what he wrote in 1850:

> The good influence of the Bible, past and present as of all religious books, rests on its religious significance . . . Men sometimes fear the Bible will be destroyed by freedom of thought and freedom of speech. Let it perish if such be the case. Truth cannot fear the light, nor are men so mad as to forsake a well of living water. All the free thinking in the world could not destroy the *Iliad*; how much less the truths of the Bible, which . . . has already endured the greatest abuse at the hands of its friends, who make it an idol, and would have all men do it homage. We need call none our master, but the Father of All. Yet the Bible, if wisely used, is still a blessed teacher. Spite of the superstition and folly of its worshippers, it has helped millions to the fountain where Moses and Jesus, with the holy hearted of all time, have stopped and been filled. We see the mistakes of its writers, for though noble and of great stature, they saw not all things. We reject their follies; but their words of truth are still before us, to admonish, to encourage, and to bless. From time to time, God raises up a prophet to lead mankind. He speaks his word as it is given him, serves his generation for the time, and falls at last, when it is expedient he should give way to the next comforter whom God shall send. But mankind is greater than a man, and never dies. The experience of the past lives in the present. The light that shone at Nineveh, Egypt, Judea, Athens, Rome, shines no more from those points; it is everywhere. Can truth decease, and a good idea once made real ever perish? Mankind, moving solemnly on its appointed road, from age to age, passed by its imperfect teachers, guided by their light, blessed by their toil, and sprinkled with their blood. But before and above us forever. (*A Discourse of Religion*)

I cannot here argue all the philosophical issues associated with interpretative method.[2] Were I to do so, we would never get to the texts themselves. I can only be straightforward about my general presuppositions. The chapters that follow will take up the whole of the Bible, using the general structure of the culturally dominant Protestant version and attempting to open up some new interpretations for skeptics, seekers, and religious liberals. Beginning at the beginning: with the first chapters of the Book of Genesis.

THE HEBREW BIBLE (OLD TESTAMENT)

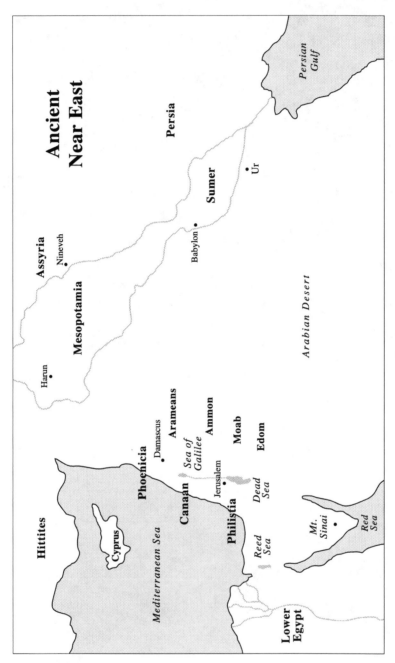

Map of ancient Near East

A BASIC CHRONOLOGY FOR THE HEBREW BIBLE

1900–1800 B.C.E.	Middle Bronze Age migrations; Setting for Abraham legends
1250–1200 B.C.E.	Era of the Exodus from Egypt
1005 B.C.E.	David establishes monarchy at Jerusalem
928 B.C.E.	Death of Solomon; division of kingdom
853 B.C.E.	King Ahab of Israel dies; era of Elijah
760–690 B.C.E.	Prophets Amos and Hosea in Israel; Prophets Isaiah and Micah in Judah
722 B.C.E.	Fall of the Northern Kingdom to Assyria; E traditions of North meet J of South
622 B.C.E.	King Josiah; "Book of the Law"(D) found
587 B.C.E.	Fall of Jerusalem
587–538 B.C.E.	Exile in Babylon
539 B.C.E.	Cyrus of Persia conquers Babylon
538 B.C.E.	First wave of the return
516 B.C.E.	Second Temple completed
450 B.C.E.	Walls of Jerusalem rebuilt by Nehemiah; Ezra has Torah read publicly; P editor
332 B.C.E.	Persian Empire defeated by Alexander
323 B.C.E.	Death of Alexander; Hellenistic Period

301 B.C.E.	Israel ruled by Ptolemaic Egypt
201 B.C.E.	Israel ruled by Seleucids of Antioch
160s B.C.E.	Maccabean Revolt; Hasmonean dynasty Book of Daniel compiled; Septuagint — Greek trans. of Bible
70 C.E.	Romans destroy Jerusalem and Temple
140 C.E.	Rabbinic canon established; Mishnah

Creations: In the Beginning
Genesis 1 to 11

Theologian Paul Tillich was fond of pointing out that, in the Bible's understanding, the Creator, in whose image we humans are said to be made, is not to be imaged, in human or any other terms drawn from creation. Therefore any image we may have of God, however traditional, however exalted, is never truly a biblical image. For the Bible, there is always a "God above God," above any God we can image or imagine.

To illustrate this, with appropriate irony, now imagine a cartoon. As I recall, it appeared in *The New Yorker* some years ago. It depicts a globe, blue and green, poised in the middle of space. On the globe, we see a prominent tree, and on the tree, a bright red apple; while around the trunk twists a serpent and beneath its boughs stand a naked man and woman. Obviously, it's the Earth, just after its mythical creation. Because, there above it all, smiling down benevolently on his handiwork, is the Creator, just as Michelangelo might have portrayed Him (sic): with long white flowing beard and long white flowing robes. But above this God, with even longer, whiter, and more flowing beard and robes, is another figure, pointing to the globe, saying to God, "And for *this* you expect a Ph.D.?"

If nothing else, this illustrates a division in our own human reactions to creation itself. Some days we feel awed by its beauty, as the psalmist did: "When I look at your heavens, the work of your fingers, the moon and the stars that you have established; what are human beings that you are mindful of them, mortals that you care for them?" (Ps. 8:3–4). Other days we think that, if only *I* had been consulted at the beginning, I might have had some suggestions for improvement to offer the Creator!

The British biologist J. B. S. Haldane was once asked what, after a lifetime of studying creation, he had been able to conclude about nature of the Creator. "God," said Haldane dryly, "seems inordinately fond of beetles."

Creation seems to be a mixture of order and freedom. The more complex the organism, the greater is its freedom, and the greater its capacity to do harm to others and to the larger order of things. The freedom is pervasive, however. Even subatomic particles have an indeterminacy. Viruses can mutate and cross species. Cells, in replicating themselves, can go wildly out of control. And human beings — well, just read the daily newspapers. No wonder the Bible has not one, but two, stories of creation — one about the creation of the cosmos and the creatures on earth, another about the creation of human beings. They come from different strands of tradition (P and J respectively) and do not entirely agree. Neither do we.

Why is there something, rather than nothing? And why are *we* here, we human beings, within the vast, incomprehensible beauty of all that exists? Only poets, not scientists, attempt to provide us with answers. "We are here to abet creation and to witness to it," writes Annie Dillard, "to notice each other's beautiful face and complex nature so that creation need not play to an empty house."

Some people think of "the beginning," creation, as an event in time. And they want to make the first chapter of Genesis a literal account of its stages. But it isn't. Nor is it a theologian's *creatio ex nihilo*, a creation out of nothing. A student once reportedly asked St. Augustine what God was doing *before* creating the heavens and the earth. The theologian was speechless for a moment, and then replied, "Creating Hell, for snips who ask me questions like that!"

Carefully read, Genesis 1 begins with matter already in existence. "In the beginning, God created the heavens and the earth." But before the beginning, it goes on to say, "The earth was without form and void, and darkness was upon the face of the deep; and the Spirit of God was moving over the face of the waters."

Never mind the inconsistency. The first chapter of Genesis is not a treatise in natural history. It is a poetic prologue to a sacred history in the form of a hymn, a liturgical poem exalting God for creating order out of primal chaos. Its six stanzas each begin with the words, "And God said . . ." ". . . Let there be light," for example, or "Let the waters bring forth . . ." Each then repeats the comment, "And God saw that it was good," and ends with the refrain, "And there was evening and there was morning, a *new* day."

People who want the biblical account of creation given "equal time" in public school classrooms along with cosmic and biological evolution have a distorted view of both science and the Bible. Genesis I "no more belongs in a high school science textbook than pages of that textbook would belong in the hymnbooks of the church," as Martin Marty puts it.

On the other hand, I once had a good friend who was a devout atheist. She handed me two books by physicists. One questioned the theory of the "Big Bang," at least as an event in time. The other suggested that chaos might be inherent in the nature of the cosmos. "See," she said, "there was no creation! And there's no 'Creator'!"

I resisted a temptation to point out that the physicists might now be *closer* to Genesis than they were before. But I knew that might mislead her. I didn't want to go only halfway in demythologizing, as some do when they treat the "days" of the text as the only metaphors, and have them stand for evolutionary epochs.

Once I even helped create a service of worship with that thesis. We used readings about creation from two sources. One set came from a poetic elaboration of the six-day creation (from James Weldon Johnson's *God's Trombones: Negro Sermons in Verse*). The other set came from scientific writers: astronomers like Carl Sagan, biologists like Lewis Thomas, anthropologists like Loren Eiseley, all expressing awe at the emergence of stars and planets, life up from the waters, and consciousness. It was effective in its way. But I'm no longer sure it did justice to the full range of differences and similarities between modern ideas of evolution and ancient ideas of creation.

It implies, for example, that both scientific and biblical creations were once-and-long-ago. That's not fair to either view. For the Bible, as for ancient myths in the Near East generally, creation was a never-ending process, linked always to *re-creation*. Creation myths did not serve primarily to fill intellectual gaps, to answer questions about where things came from. They had a more immediate and vital function. They celebrated the Divine, bringing order out of primal chaos, but *they did not assume that the Chaos went away.*[1]

Quite the contrary: the potential for disorder and chaos, both in nature's rhythms and in human society, remained close at hand. Chanting or reciting the creation myths played an important role in evoking how the tenuous order in which human beings live might be sustained and renewed. The God who is praised as Creator is one who re-creates as well, upholding and reinforcing the rhythms, patterns, structures, and creativity that make life possible in the first place. So no wonder the creation story ends by establishing a day of worship, the Sabbath rest.[2]

On the seventh day, as we start a second chapter, God rests from it all, and a transition is made to a second story of creation. The transition isn't a very smooth one. Early biblical scholars noticed that long ago. The Creator is now not just *Elohim*, as in the hymn, but *Yahweh Elohim*. In the hymn, after creating the plants and other animals, "*Elohim* created humankind (*adam*) in his image; in the image of God he created them; male and female he created them" (Gen. 1:27). But here, even before plants arise, the male of our species is formed first, made from mother earth:

"In the day that the LORD God (*Yahweh Elohim*) made the earth and heavens, when no plant of the field was yet in the earth and no herb of the field had yet sprung up—for the LORD God had not caused it to rain upon the earth, and there was no man to till the ground; but a mist went up from the earth and watered the whole face of the ground—then the LORD God formed man (*adam*) from the dust (*adamah*) of the ground, and breathed into his nostrils the breath of life; and *adam* became a living being" (Gen. 2:5–7).

God is both beyond gender and male here. So is "man." Woman appears first as an equal in creation, but then in the second version of creation, as the "second sex." In the world as we know it, new life comes from the female body. But in this second story, Eve is portrayed as emerging from the body of Adam—made from a rib. Why, we ask, does the Bible make this shift?

One answer is simple: Just as the hymn to creation is used to rationalize the liturgical practice of Sabbath rest, God becomes male here, and woman the second sex, because that rationalizes the ethos of a patriarchal society. But it is also worth noting that the typical Near Eastern creation myths were much more sexualized than the biblical accounts. They had to do with the male sky god impregnating the female earth goddess. There are vestiges here. *Adam* emerges from *adamah*, mother earth, after it is watered, not from on high, but from below, by a mist or a spring. But then the Creator takes on female roles, acting like both a potter and a midwife, shaping a creature from dust, blowing into its nostrils the breath of life.

Yet there is no question that the Bible associates God more with the male sky god than with the earth goddess. I won't claim that his reading challenges all the sexism in that basic polarity, but literary critic Northrop Frye, in his book *The Great Code: The Bible and Literature,* connects this choice to the fact that these myths of creation are a prologue to a sacred and open-ended history, and not to a series of myths about the cycles of nature. "The maleness of God," he writes, "seems to be connected with the Bible's resistance to the notion of a containing cycle of fate or inevitability as the highest category that our minds can conceive." The point about the creation of Eve from Adam's rib, suggests the text, is that the two are to be considered "one flesh." A man is to leave his own parents and be united to his wife (Gen. 2:24). Marriage, as we shall see, among the Hebrews was at first matrilocal: the man going to live with his wife's family. In order to be born at all, Frye points out, much less do such leaving, it is the mother we have to leave. The larger mother, Nature, however, admits of no real separations. We are born, we die, and everything is contained within Mother Nature, in whom there are no real endings, or beginnings. But for the Hebrews, the whole point of this beginning (Genesis) was to introduce a history, an open-ended story, not one that was only a part of a cycle. In the creation hymn, after all, the central metaphor for "beginning" is not really birth at all, but rather dawn and waking: "And it was morning and evening, a new day."

Admittedly, this is "still contained within a cycle: we know that at the end of the day we shall return to the world of sleep, but in the meantime there is a sense of self-transcendence, of consciousness getting 'up' from an unreal into a real, or at least a more real, world," writes Frye. "The Greek thinker Heraclitus refers to this . . . as a passing from a world where everyone has his or her own 'logos' into a world where there is a common 'logos.' Genesis presents the Creation as a sudden coming into being of a world through articulate speech (another aspect of logos), conscious perception, light and stability."[3]

Another form of awakening is that of humankind from animality to self-consciousness, symbolized by clothing, sexual self-awareness, and "the knowledge of good and evil." Self-consciousness and moral choice are both founded on a consciousness of facing an objective environment containing both the possibility of death and the inevitability of mortality. These realities are given dramatic form in the third chapter of Genesis. Theology changes this story from one of a human rise to consciousness into "the fall of man" through disobedience to a divine command.

In naturalistic mythologies, death is not seen as a problem, just as part of the cycle. But nature is one thing, the human experience of time and history another. In the latter, we often experience death as *unnat-ural*, so that if we die, someone or something must be to blame. Here the blame is not on God. Creation is good; so is the Creator. And made in God's image, humankind was not meant to die.

The folk mythology of the ancient Near East was full of tales aimed at explaining how humanity once had immortality but was cheated out of it by frightened or malicious divinities. Frye notes that "the Genesis account permits itself a verse (chapter 3, verse 22), in which God seems to be telling other gods that man is now 'one of us'— in a position to threaten their power unless they do something about it at once, with a break in the syntax that suggests genuine terror." The malicious char-acter, however, is the serpent, whose ability to shed its skin is a symbol of immortality in the natural world. But nowhere is the serpent, as in later interpretations, identified with the Accuser in the heavenly court, the Satan, or *diabolos*.

Despite the themes of death and judgment, it would also be a mistake for us to read into Genesis 3 any more elaborate theological doctrine of "original sin," of human depravity, or of all nature being marred by hu-man disobedience, as Milton drew the story in *Paradise Lost*. Jewish tra-dition finds no such dark doctrine there; just a realistic portrayal of our human proclivity to misuse the freedom that God gives us.

In her book, *Adam, Eve and the Serpent,* Elaine Pagels argues that in the first three Christian centuries, that's how early Christians in-terpreted the story as well. But then things changed. Because they honored chastity and virginity in a way that contrasted with pagan so-ciety, Christian interpretations of Genesis gradually began to iden-tify sin with sexuality. Another shift came in the realm of politics. It was one thing to emphasize free will and moral choice during a time of Christian persecution and martyrdom. But once the emperors were Christian, the church an established religion, theologians noticed that Christian rulers could be just as corrupt and cruel as pagans. A darker view of human nature suddenly had much to commend it. Augustine denied that human beings even had the power *not* to sin.[4]

Christian interpretations of the problematic beginning of human history, however, can only be understood fairly in relation to its doctrines of subsequent salvation. These point to a resolution in the "Second Adam," Christ, and, for Catholics, in the "Second Eve," Mary.[5] Jewish tradition resolves the human tendency to abuse free choice through the gift of ever clearer commandments about how to stay in right relationship with God and one another. One *midrash*, for example, far from blaming Eve for tasting the apple, blames Adam for distorting God's one simple command by being paternalistic toward her. He embellishes, telling her not only not to eat, but not to touch, lest she die. When she sees the serpent touch the tree without harm, she concludes that Adam was mistaken and takes the fatal bite.

The rabbis knew that blaming doesn't help. One bemused response to this theme is captured in some modern light verse:

> I've thought it all over. What could it have been?
> What was it really — original sin?
> Was it pride, disobedience, envy, or lust?
> Or gluttony, arrogance, greed, breech of trust?
> Intellectual pride, ambition for glory?
> None quite seems to fit the true facts of the story.
> When the question was asked, "Who has disobeyed?"
> Did each one acknowledge the part he had played?
> Adam, true gentleman right from the start,
> Lost not a moment disclaiming his part.
> "'T was not I," said he. "I was pleased with my diet.
> That woman you gave me, she forced me to try it."
> And Eve? "'T was the serpent who promised so much —
> That the fruit was sweet-tasting and pleasant to touch —
> Of all the fruits in the garden the most healthful kind,
> Warming the heart and expanding the mind."

And the serpent? "I played on their weaknesses — true,
But the weaknesses there were created by you."
Original sin? Still with us, worse luck.
The original sin was passing the buck!

(Ann Schultz, "Doggerel on a Theme by Milton")[6]

After the story of the Fall, as it is traditionally called, Genesis goes on to recount other early legends of human misdoing. During and after the Exile the Priestly editors wove these together. They combined their own contributions (such as the opening hymn) with materials inherited from both the southern Yahwist and northern Elohist traditions. The goal was to place the story of Israel in perspective by preceding it with the legendary tales of ancestors going back all the way to the origin of creation. The book they created falls into four main parts:

I.   The Primeval History, Chapters 1 through 11.
II. The Abraham and Sarah Legends, Chapters 12 to 24.
III. The Legends of Jacob (Israel), Chapters 25 to 35.
IV. The Story of Joseph, Chapters 37 through 50.

Many readers of the material in Genesis notice how many stories of injustice and violence abound in the primeval legends. Harvard law professor Alan M. Dershowitz, in his book *The Genesis of Justice*, argues that the very trial-and-error, inconsistent, and experiential nature of divine justice in the book of Genesis is designed to be a prelude to the more systematic law of the Ten Commandments when they appear in the next book, Exodus.[7]

Take the story of Cain murdering his brother, Abel. One cleric I know once wrote a more "acceptable" version in which the brothers fight but then shake hands and make up! Anyone who knows the more murderous elements of sibling rivalry was surely unconvinced. In fact, the story portrays what must have been a real tension in ancient society: between those who tilled the ground, like Cain, and those who kept flocks, like Abel.

Throughout Genesis God seems to show favor to the younger sibling over the elder, and so responds to Abel's offerings but not to Cain's. Then Yahweh says to Cain, "Why are you angry, and why has your countenance fallen? If you do well, will you not be accepted? And if you do not do well, sin is crouching at the door . . ."

In John Steinbeck's novel *East of Eden,* the characters debate how the next phrase should be translated. Five Chinese men spend two years studying Hebrew, just to resolve whether God said, "Sin crouches at the door but *thou shalt* rule over it," as in the KJV, or whether God said, "Do thou rule over it," as the American Standard Bible has it.

"After two years, they decided that both translations were wrong. The true meaning of God's word *timshol* was 'Thou mayest rule over it.'" Mr. Lee says, "Don't you see? The American Standard *orders* men to triumph over sin. The King James makes a *promise* in 'thou shalt.' But the Hebrew 'thou mayest' gives us a choice. It might be the most important word in the Bible!"[8]

As readers of these stories, we can easily become upset not only with the fallible choices of the human beings involved but also with the reported reactions of their Creator. Yahweh seems quite inconsistent— alternately soft on some crimes and overreactive to others. Adam and Eve are told, for example, that the punishment for eating from the tree will be death itself. Instead, what they get is simply exile from the garden. Likewise, Cain is not killed for murdering his brother. The mark he is given, in fact, is for his protection!

The rabbis sometimes accounted for the tension in the stories by seeing God as a mixture of justice and mercy. Interestingly, they associated God as judge with Elohim and God as merciful with the divine name, YHWH. The first story in Genesis that intermingles those two terms is the story of the Flood in Genesis 6–9.

Human beings have continued to murder one another. Blood cries out from the ground. Rather than punish individuals, God seems to overreact, choosing to cleanse the earth by sending a flood upon the whole planet. He sends a warning to only one just man, Noah, telling him to save his family and a male and female of every species.

This legend derives from Mesopotamian sources like the epic of Gilgamesh. The hero there sets out in search of eternal life and finds a man named Ut-Napishtim, who has the secret and tells his story. He was king of a Sumerian city at the time of a great (regional, not global) flood, and rode it out in a large ship. Gilgamesh obtains the secret of eternal life from him, nearly fulfills the conditions, but then makes mistakes and loses the secret.

In the biblical story, God repents of having overreacted and promises not to do it again, placing the rainbow in the sky as the sign of that covenant. Finally, he establishes more proportional limits to universal justice, saying, "I will require a reckoning for human life. Whoever sheds the blood of a human, by a human shall that person's blood be shed; for in his own image God made humankind" (Gen. 9:6). This is frequently taken out of context, forgetting subsequent commands to forgive, to justify the death penalty. It is followed by the instruction, also often taken out of context, to "be fruitful and multiply." While many Catholics resist the death penalty, they join with Mormons in treating this early level of the tradition as though it were a command-ment still in full force and effect. Others of us, taking what could be called a more environmental interpretation of the Flood, warn against human overpopulation.

The story ends with Noah as the first cultivator of a vineyard—and the first drunk. His sons Shem, Japeth, and Ham are the ancestors of the Semites of the Middle East (including the Hebrews), of Caucasians (Japeth), and of Canaanites, Egyptians, and Africans (Ham). Ham sees his father naked, sleeping it off. "When Noah awoke from his wine and knew what his youngest son had done to him, he said, 'Cursed be Canaan; lowest of slaves shall he be to his brothers.' " And so the curse of racism enters the story.[9]

Why *are* human beings divided into different tribes and nations and linguistic groups? One approach is to see the question as part of a larger puzzle about Creation itself. I'm reminded of an old story that involves some inebriation. At a cocktail party, a rationalist in his cups goes up to a woman who is both a poet and a theologian. "Why did God make so *much* of everything?" he demands. "There's just too much! Too many stars, too many species, too many people, too many languages and reli-gions! Wouldn't just one language and religion have been better?"

"Perhaps God was a little drunk," the woman replies.

"Drunk?" said the rationalist. "What could get the Creator of the Universe inebriated?"

"Perhaps it was Love," she opines.

Of course Genesis explains all the linguistic divisions and confusions of humankind rather differently. A primeval linguistic unity is presumed. Then Genesis 11 has human arrogance misuse that unity to build a Tower in Babel reaching up toward heaven. There is a bad pun or false etymology here, playing on the Hebrew word for confusion, *balal,* and the name of the city with the great tower: *Bab-ilu,* meaning "the gate of God." As it happens, there was a large tower, or *ziggurat,* in Babylon, left unfinished by an early Sumerian king, as well as a huge, complete one, formed in seven stages, one for each planet and day of the week, built by Nebuchadnezzar in the seventh century B.C.E. One way to read this story is as an early reaction of a poor, marginalized people — the Hebrews — against the tendency of all empires toward cultural hegemony and linguistic uniformity.

The Hebrews had reason to think of Mesopotamia ambivalently. It was a source of conquering empires in their history. But it was also a source of much of the mythic material in their culture and the legendary homeland of their ancient ancestor, Abraham. And it is to the legends of Abraham and his progeny that we now turn. Among other things, they were used to explain the relationships between the Israelites and the other neighboring peoples of the ancient Near East.

Generations:
Matriarchs, Patriarchs, and Children
Genesis 12 to 50

Why do we say "the God of Abraham, the God of Isaac, the God of Jacob and our God"? "Because God must be encountered anew in every generation." So said the Hasidic sages.[1] Or why might we say "the God of Sarah, the God of Rebekah, the God of Rachel, and our God?" ask modern Jewish feminists. "Because we *are* encountering God anew in *our* generation!"

The legends of the patriarchs and matriarchs of Israel are not just ancient family stories, though they certainly are that. They had many functions, not the least of which was to explain relationships within and beyond the tribes of Israel. But how shall we, in an era that radically critiques patriarchy, read the stories that are so clearly about an entire culture of patriarchs, their wives, and their children?

One interpretation of the ancient history of the Near East has tried to suggest that *before* patriarchy there was an earlier, more peaceful, nurturing, and matriarchal agricultural era that was pushed aside by a more violent, competitive, male-dominated, nomadic form of society represented by these stories. Alas, even if these stories do represent the latter, the notion of prehistoric matriarchy seems more and more to be a chimera. In her book *The Myth of Matriarchal Prehistory: Why an Invented Past Won't Give Women a Future,* feminist anthropologist Cynthia Eller shows that neither the archeological evidence nor the understandable desire for a matriarchal Eden justifies the notion. Without attempting to recapitulate all her argument or her evidence here, suffice it to say that patriarchal dominance seems very ancient indeed. In ancient Mesopotamia, even where female goddesses were worshiped, feminist historians now also find the evidence of female subordination, slavery, and child sacrifice.[2]

Judaism, Islam, and Christianity alike see Abraham as their common spiritual forebear, the founder of Western monotheism. His original name is Abram, meaning "the father is exalted." Later it is changed to

Abraham, "the father of many." With his own father, Terah, his wife, Sarai (later Sarah), and his nephew, Lot, he has left their original home in the southern part of Mesopotamia, in Ur, to go live in the city of upper Mesopotamia associated with his brother, Haran. There he feels the call of the high god, El, telling him to leave his father's household and go forth to a land he will be shown, where he will become himself the father of a great nation and a blessing to the world. Going to Canaan, they follow the arc of the Near East's "Fertile Crescent." After a time of famine takes them further, into Egypt, he returns to Canaan. Behind all this may lie memories of historic migrations in the Middle Bronze Age, circa 2000–1800 B.C.E.

Entering Egypt, Abram decides to declare that the beautiful Sarai is his sister, not his wife, and let the Egyptians have her if they want her, rather than risk being killed for her. Plagues fall on Pharaoh for taking another man's wife and he rebukes Abram (Gen. 12). By the time they leave Egypt, Abram is rich, but Sarah is well past bearing children and has given Abram her Egyptian servant, Hagar, as a substitute in the begetting of an heir, and Hagar has given birth to Ishmael. Abram has made a covenant with El, the sign of which is circumcision, and been renamed (Gen. 15–17).

Circumcision was both an Egyptian custom and a Semitic marriage ritual to ward off evil. The *Anchor Bible Dictionary* says that "the authors of Genesis 17 lived in a culture, probably during the Exile, which did not practice circumcision. They had to explain why Israelites should circumcise their children. They drew gladly upon traditions which claimed that circumcision ensured many offspring who would be blessed by God and who would experience what God was doing for his people. Before Abraham's circumcision Sarah is not fertile; afterward she is. Before his circumcision Abraham can only beget Ishmael; afterward he can beget Isaac, the child blessed by God."[3]

In Genesis 18, three strangers visit Abraham and Sarah at their camp near the oaks of Mamre. Sarah laughs from behind the tent when they tell Abraham that she will have a son within the year. When she does give birth, they name the boy Isaac, meaning "laughter."

This story always reminds me of an actual experience my wife, Gwen, and I had visiting a Bedouin family in the southern desert of Israel, the Negev. Only the males — four generations of them — entertained us. The women were all kept out of sight. When Gwen asked where they were, she was told that strangers might want them, and that she was an "honorary male" as a guest. She was not amused. After food and coffee, the patriarch recited family stories and genealogy (their "begats"). When we bid them farewell, we finally saw the women — giggling behind a cooking tent!

What happens to Isaac, the long-awaited, beloved son, is no laughing matter, however. Many find it one of the most disturbing stories in the whole canon of the Hebrew Bible. But perhaps the only way for some of us to approach this terrifying story is, in part, through a humorous version. So I turn to the version that Woody Allen claims was found on a scroll, stuffed in a clay jar in the desert — along with two unexplained tickets to the Ice Show. The repeated use of the word "Oldsmobile" in some of these scrolls has some to doubt their authenticity, but here's the part about Abraham and Isaac:[4]

> ... And Abraham awoke in the middle of the night and said to his ... son, Isaac, "I have had a dream where the voice of the Lord sayeth that I must sacrifice thou, so put your pants on."
>
> And Isaac trembled and said, "So what did you say? I mean when He brought this whole thing up?"
>
> "What am I going to say?" Abraham said. "I'm standing there at two A.M. in my underwear with the Creator of the Universe. Should I argue?" ...
>
> And Sarah who heard Abraham's plan grew vexed and said, "How doth thou know it was the Lord and not, say, thy friend who loveth practical jokes ... ?"
>
> And Abraham answered, "Because ... it was a deep, resonant voice, well modulated, and nobody in the desert can get a rumble in it like that." ...
>
> And so he took Isaac to a certain place and prepared to sacrifice him but at the last minute the Lord stayed Abraham's hand and said, "How could thou doest such a thing?"
>
> And Abraham said, "But thou said–"
>
> "Never mind what I said," the Lord spake. "Doth thou listen to every crazy idea that comes thy way?" And Abraham grew ashamed ...

"I jokingly suggest thou sacrifice Isaac and thou immediately runs out to do it."

And Abraham fell to his knees, "See, I never know when you're kidding."

And the Lord thundered, "No sense of humor! I can't believe it!"

"But doth this not prove I love thee, that I was willing to donate mine only son on thy whim?"

And the Lord said, "It proves that some men will follow any order no matter how asinine as long as it comes from a resonant, well-modulated voice."

Let's face it: This whole story shocks our modern sensibilities. Yet serious interpretation of it has been important to all three great monotheistic religions.

Christians have read this near-sacrifice as anticipating the actual death of God's own beloved son, Jesus. Abraham's faith in God, accounted to him as righteousness according to Genesis 15:6, is particularly praised in the Pauline tradition (Rom. 4:3; Gal. 3:6). Kierkegaard, in *Fear and Trembling,* sees Abraham's obedience as an example of faith overruling ethics.

The Koran is ambiguous about which of his sons Ibrahim takes out to sacrifice, but Muslim tradition says that it was not Isaac but Ishmael, ancestor of the Arabs, who in the Hebrew Bible is cast out into the desert, along with his mother, Hagar, after Isaac is born to Sarah. Islam calls the event the *Kurban* and associates it with Mecca, where Ishmael is said to have helped his father Abraham to clear away the pagan idols and build the Ka'aba as the place to worship Allah as the only God.

Judaism calls this story the *Akedah,* or Binding, of Isaac. It is the scripture passage read at the New Year, Rosh Hashanah. Jewish tradition identifies the place to which Isaac is taken, Mount Moriah, with the Temple Mount in Jerusalem, and in fact with the stone under the Al Aqsa Mosque ("The Dome of the Rock") in Jerusalem.

But competing interpretations among the children of Abraham are only one reason that many social critics simply detest this story. Carol Delaney, in her book *Abraham on Trial: The Social Legacy of Biblical Myth,* charges it with an entire legacy of patriarchal child abuse, and worse. Others, however, read the whole story "against the grain" and

believe that its purpose was to put an end to the all-too-common practice of sacrificing children to the gods, by saying dramatically, "Our
God does not want that!"[5]

In the ancient world, the first fruits of the earth, and of the flocks,
were seen as subject to sacrifice in order to ensure fertility (cf. the offerings of Cain and Abel). So were children. The Bible later says, "You
shall set apart to the Lord all that first opens the womb. All the firstborn of your livestock that are males shall be the Lord's. But . . . every
first-born male among your children you shall redeem," and not sacrifice (Exod. 12: 12–13).

Patriarchy may be oppressive. But its emergence in human history
seems to have had a good deal to do with getting men to accept responsibility as fathers for their offspring, despite anxieties about the true
paternity of the firstborn. Did those three strangers, after all, have anything to do with Sarah finally getting pregnant and laughing?[6]

The Bible condemns the nearby Edomites for sacrificing children
to their god, Moloch—a name related to the Semitic word for king,
melek. Yet even Hebrews did this, especially in time of war. Jeremiah
denounces the practice during the siege of Jerusalem. Yet perhaps we
should not be too smug. After all, we *still* sacrifice our sons to the war
god, Moloch!

In Genesis 22, Isaac is not sacrificed. A ram appears at the last minute,
provided by God, as Abraham had told his son would happen. Throughout the stories of the patriarchal generations, we find a sub-theme of
substitutions: Hagar as a substitute for Sarah, Isaac for Ishmael. When
Isaac and his wife Rebekah themselves have twin sons, the mother substitutes her favorite, the second-born, Jacob, for Esau (ancestor of the
Edomites). Jacob's name is related to the word "heel," since he is depicted as having held on to his brother's heel when they were born, and
to the word for "cheat," since he cheats Esau of his birth-right and of
their father's blessing (Gen. 25, 27).

More substitutions lie ahead and the cheater is cheated. When Jacob
flees his brother's wrath, he goes to his mother's brother to obtain a
wife. This pattern of going to the mother's uncle for a wife, by the way,
is typical of a society that is both matrilineal and matrilocal. Orthodox
Judaism still traces Jewish belonging through the mother. But the Jacob
stories mark a break between the matrilocal practice of an agricultural

society and that of more nomadic herders. Jacob works for his uncle Laban for seven years, only to have the older sister, Leah, substituted for the younger, Rachel, on the wedding night. He then works seven more years. When he breaks with matrilocal practice by leaving with his wives and children and herds, he has an encounter with God like an encounter with conscience.

God is sometimes *heard* in these stories, but is never directly *seen*.[7] God may send dreams, or angelic beings as messengers. Jacob's first encounter with God had come while fleeing from Esau. He lay down to sleep with nothing but a stone for a pillow. He dreams about ladderlike steps up to heaven, with divine messengers going up and down. These steps may be a deliberate contrast with the humanly constructed Tower of Babel, a symbol of pride. In any case, when he awakes, he says, "Surely the Holy is in this place, and I did not know it!" Then he sets stone upon stone and dedicates the very first place set aside for worship in the Bible, calling it Beth El, the "House of God." Finally, he dedicates himself, saying one tenth, a tithe, of everything he has he will give to God (Gen. 28).[8]

Leaving Laban, Jacob has another memorable spiritual experience by night. At the ford of the River Jabbok, the boundary between Laban's and Esau's lands, he meets a divine being, or messenger, with whom he must wrestle. He persists all through the night, and, though he also gets his hip dislocated, wins both a blessing and a new name — Israel, meaning "One who struggles with God" (Gen. 32).

Through his wives, Rachel and Leah, and their two maids, Zilpah and Bilhah, Jacob/Israel becomes the father of twelve sons and of all the tribes of Israel. The differing mothers may be attempts to explain how the later twelve-tribe confederation came to have internal subgroupings.

There is only one daughter, Dinah, about whom a horrific story is told in Genesis 34. Author Anita Diamant has written a brilliant extended *midrash* on this story in a novel written from the point of view of Dinah, *The Red Tent*. It's a good example of how a feminist consciousness can use even a "text of terror" from among these ancient and patriarchal stories, by reading them imaginatively and "against the grain."[9]

In the Dinah story, the eldest sons, Reuben and Levi, lose their father's favor. So does Judah, for his misdeeds toward his daughter-in-law, Tamar. So when the story opens, Jacob's favor has shifted to his eleventh son, the youngest at that time, Joseph, who becomes the central character in a twelve-chapter novella that occupies the entire remainder of Genesis. So engaging is the Joseph story that it has been retold by novelist Thomas Mann (*Joseph and His Brothers*) and in a musical, *Joseph and the Amazing Technicolor Dreamcoat*.

The Joseph story follows the motif of the "death and resurrection of the beloved son," a pattern that Jewish scholar Jon Levenson has identified as central to the whole Bible. Certainly it appears in the stories of Isaac, Jacob, Joseph, and, finally, Jesus.[10]

As the favorite son of his father's old age, Joseph has been given a beautiful robe, or "coat of many colors." He is also impolitic enough to tell his brothers that he has dreamed of eleven sheaves of wheat bowing down to his sheaf, and of the sun and the moon and the eleven stars bowing down to him. His jealous brothers strip him of his coat, throw him into a pit, sell him to slave traders bound for Egypt, dip the coat in blood, and tell their father that Joseph has been devoured by a wild beast.

One obvious purpose of the story in the biblical narrative is to answer the question, "How did the children of Israel come to be slaves in Egypt?" The answer is that, like Abraham before them, they went there searching for food in a time of famine in Canaan. By that time, Joseph has survived numerous trials and has been placed in virtual charge of the kingdom by Pharaoh.

As a servant in the household of the noble Potiphar, Joseph meets his first test by resisting the sexual advances of Potiphar's wife. Then he uses his abilities as a dreamer and an interpreter of dreams to win the favor of Pharaoh himself. Having seen in a dream seven fat cattle and seven thin ones, he predicts that seven abundant harvests will be followed by seven lean years. Pharaoh puts him in charge of storing grain. When his brothers, who do not recognize him, come in search of grain, Joseph makes it appear that the new favorite, his younger brother, Benjamin, has stolen, and demands that he be left behind as a hostage until old Jacob/Israel himself comes to Egypt. Finally all his brothers are forced to say, in front of their father, "We are here as *your* slaves!" Only then does the redeemed slave, Joseph, present his Egyptian-born sons, Manasseh and Ephraim, to be blessed by their grandfather. Jacob dies in Egypt, but not before Joseph has promised to bury him back in the Promised Land. Which brings us to the story that was central to the self-understanding of the Hebrews — their exodus from Egypt and their profound sense of gratitude and responsibility before the God who saw to their liberation.

Liberations: The Exodus and the Wandering in the Wilderness

According to one story of the Bible's interpretation, a boy once came home from Sunday school. "Well, what did you learn?" his father asked.

"How the people of Israel were kept in Egypt and used as slaves by this Pharaoh dude."

"Oh?" said the father. "Then what happened?"

"A guy named Moses tried all these special effects on 'em. Really neat: turned the river to blood, covered 'em with frogs, and bugs, and boils, beat 'em down with hailstones, and locusts, and scared 'em with an eclipse and killin' their cattle and killin' their kids."

"Did it work?"

"Well, Pharaoh lets 'em go, but then he sends his army after 'em."

"And then?"

"Well . . . Moses calls in the Israeli air force. And they strafe the Egyptian tanks and destroy 'em on the ground and give cover while the engineers lay down this pontoon bridge across the Red Sea. And then the people of Israel cross over without gettin' their feet wet. But when the Egyptian army gets on the pontoon bridge, the air force comes back and bombs it away, and the Egyptians drown."

"Is *that* what your teacher told you?"

"Well, not exactly. But if I told it the way *she* did, you'd say I was makin' the whole thing up!"

Perhaps you have seen the Cecil B. DeMille version of the story, *The Ten Commandments*, or the more recent Disney film *The Prince of Egypt*. If you have ever taken part in a Passover Seder, you have heard it not only recited, but questioned and interpreted anew. The influence of the story of Israel's liberation from Egypt is not just on pop culture and on religious memory, however. It is so central to the Bible, and therefore to Western thought, that interpretations of the Exodus have influenced political and social movements from the Puritans and the founding of America through Marxism to every contemporary liberation movement.

As we have it in the Bible, the story was given mythic drama as old oral traditions were turned into national epic. The ten plagues said to have befallen Egypt are good examples. So is the parting of the waters. Probably the number of people involved was exaggerated. The Bible says there were 600,000 Israelite men, plus their families, making millions. Many modern scholars, however, believe that only a portion of the later twelve-tribe people of Israel actually went through the Exodus experience. But beneath the mythic lies a very powerful and understandable human story, likely grounded in some actuality of history.

It may help us understand the Exodus to be reminded that, like all stories, this one has a beginning (Egypt), a middle (Wilderness), and an end (entry into the Promised Land). And no part can be understood apart from the others, especially not the first transition, the miraculous parting of the Red Sea. Reductionists will try to explain the matter simply: the Israelites left Egypt *north* of the Red Sea, crossing the *Reed* Sea, a marshy area where the Suez Canal now flows. Pharaoh's chariots just couldn't follow.

In his engaging best-seller *Walking the Bible: A Journey by Land Through the Five Books of Moses,* journalist Bruce Feiler takes this approach. But geography should perhaps interest us less than *midrashim* that comment on the story of the waters parting.

One *midrash* says that when Moses raised his staff above the waters to make them part, at first nothing happened. Only when the first of the Israelites actually stepped *into* the dangerous waters did they divide. A feminist *midrash* says that person was a woman — perhaps Miriam, the sister of Moses, whose song on reaching the other side is the ancient hymn of exaltation in Exodus 15 around which the whole complex of legends seems to gather. Still another tradition says that only when Israelites followed, entering the dangerous waters and swimming as far as they could, only then did God intervene.

The meaning is clear: no escape was possible when only fear of the Egyptians was the motivation. Fear had to be supplanted by faith, not so much in oneself or in God as in the very possibility, the promise, of a better life. What follows, however, is not immediate entry into the

Promised Land of milk and honey. It never is. In between lies the heart of the story, in the Wilderness.

Existentially, its core is something like this: however their freedom is won, the people experience great gratitude. It is as though a Voice speaks to them out of their own thanksgiving, saying, "Don't ever treat any one the way you were treated back in Egypt, and don't treat one another that way either." This voice they attribute to the god Yahweh, of whom more in a moment. Through it, they become a people.

The term "Hebrew" first appears in the Bible in the Joseph stories. It may be related to the term *Habiru* or *Hapiru* that appears in ancient Near Eastern writings of the fourteenth to eleventh centuries B.C.E. and seems to designate, not a people related by blood, but simply fugitives, outcasts, rebels — people living outside the established structures of authority. The first non-biblical use of the term "Israel," on the other hand, lies in an inscription of the Pharaoh Mer-ni-ptah (1224–1211 B.C.E.). And that name, you'll recall, means "one who *struggles* with God."

For in the story, the gratitude of the people is hardly unmixed. This is, after all, the Wilderness, the harsh and rocky desert of Sinai. Many are frightened. The water of the desert is scarce and bitter. There is little to eat. Many of them yearn for the safety and security of slave rations. Even when sweet water springing from the rock is miraculously given, they still murmur about how once they had sat by the fleshpots of Egypt and eaten bread to the full. Quails are found at twilight, and in the morning *"manna."* The word means, "what is it?" But it's described as "a fine flake-like substance, fine as hoarfrost on the ground," and often explained as a honeylike extrusion from a certain desert shrub. Yet still the people murmur against Yahweh, and against Moses and Aaron.

I remember the year my daughter's fifth-grade Sunday school class studied these stories. One week they marched through the parish hall, where their parents were gathered for an adult forum. They were all carrying placards and protest signs with inscriptions like, "Impeach Moses!" "Meat, not Manna!" "Back to Egypt!" After demonstrating, the next week they put Moses on trial. I'm sorry to report that he was soon convicted. Back to Egypt!

It was ever thus. Just ask any religious leader who has ever tried to get a group to give up the familiar to live in the challenging adventure of a real Exodus faith. Such a faith, by the way, is always concerned not only with one's *own* freedom, but also with the liberation of others from oppression. In this tradition the sense of covenant and mission are intertwined, especially when they are resisted as they are during the murmurings that arise in the Wilderness. So anyone who wants to separate "religion" and "politics" entirely should ponder the Exodus again.

The Hebrews are described as having come down to Egypt the way Latin Americans and other immigrants have come up to the United States: driven by want in their own land. Not as chattel slaves, in the sense that they were actually bought and sold. They did farm work in irrigated fields belonging to others. They did forced labor in construction: "They built for Pharaoh store cities, Pithom and Raames" (Exod. 1:11). Perhaps they also built tombs, since Egyptian religion was almost obsessed with immortality and life after death; even temples, since temples controlled the granaries.

In any case, the religion of the Hebrews takes on many characteristics that are in sharp contrast to their experience in Egypt: little concern about life after death, more about ethical treatment of others, including strangers; a God who is beyond nature and who cannot be imaged by any aspect of the creation; a founder, Moses, who is not only not divine, nor immortal, but does not even live to see them enter the Promised Land, and who is buried not under a pyramid, but in an unknown place.

In his last book, *Moses and Monotheism,* Sigmund Freud tried to argue that Moses borrowed the idea of monotheism from a religious reform undertaken under Pharaoh Akhenaton in the mid-1300s B.C.E. But what Akhenaton did was simply make exclusive the worship of Aton, the solar sun disk, and centralize worship and taxes under one powerful priesthood. There is a vast difference between an exclusive sun god and a God who not only has no part in the created order, but who created all of it. And in the story, Moses is depicted as having encountered Yahweh not in Egypt itself, but while taking refuge among the Midianites, who inhabited Sinai and northwest Arabia.

The events of the Exodus are easiest to place in the century after Akhenaton. The pharaoh "who knew not Joseph," may have been Seti, whose very name means "death," or the great builder, Ramses II (1290–1224). The pharaoh who let the children of Israel go may have been Ramses or his successor, whose inscription, as I said, mentions Israel. In any case, the divine pharaoh is replaced as their suzerain not by the man Moses, but by the god Yahweh.

The covenant at Sinai has the form of a treaty. "I am Yahweh, your God, who brought you out of the land of Egypt, out of the house of bondage. You shall have no other gods before me" (Exod. 20:2–3). Its further provisions are conditions under which Yahweh agrees to rule over and protect the people: to make no graven image, nor take the name of Yahweh in vain; to keep the Sabbath, to honor one's father and mother; not to kill, steal, or commit adultery; not to bear false witness, or covet one's neighbor's goods.

"If you obey my voice and keep my covenant," Yahweh tells Moses to tell the people, "you shall be my treasured possession out of all the peoples. Indeed, the whole earth is mine, but you shall be for me a priestly kingdom and a holy nation" (Exod. 19:5–6).

It may be that Moses first became acquainted with the name Yahweh for God when he married the daughter of a Midianite priest named Jethro, whose God dwelt on a sacred mountain. In this strand of the narrative it is called Mount Horeb. But in the overall story it is identified with Sinai, "the mountain of God." While tending his father-in-law's flocks on its slopes Moses hears his call and commission as a prophet. Out of a bush that seems to burn but not to be consumed he hears a Voice that identifies itself as with the god of his ancestors, Abraham, Isaac, and Jacob.

"I have seen the affliction of my people," says the Voice, "and have heard their cry because of their task-masters. I know their sufferings, and I have come down to deliver them out of the hand of the Egyptians. And to bring them up out of that land unto . . . a land flowing with milk and honey, unto the place of the Canaanites, and the Hittites, and the Amorites, and the Perizzites, and the Hivites and the Jebusites" (Exod. 3:7–8).

But if Yahweh is originally the god of the Midianites, and of their mountain, this concern for the Israelites reveals a dramatically larger scope. In fact, it seems that the name Yahweh is grammatically connected to the Semitic verb meaning "to be" or "to become." But this is a derived meaning, from an even more ancient root word meaning "to fall," or "to blow." Yahweh may then originally have been the Midianite name for the one who causes the rain or lightning to fall, or the wind to blow; the typical Near Eastern sky-god, in other words. But Yahweh tells Moses his name means "I am that I am," or perhaps "I will be what I will be" or even, "I am the one who brings into being." No wonder this God proves stronger than any Egyptian god of the Nile or the sun. This Yahweh is the transcendent Creator.

To be sure, at times the Israelites were to revert to worshiping Yahweh only as their tribal version of the thunder god, their Ba'al, their talisman of national and natural security. But the sense of a special covenant with the universal God is *not* a call to special privilege for Israel. It is *a call to special responsibility,* as a moral example to other peoples.

That is why so many traditional *midrashim* depict God as a kind of salesman, hawking his commandments around the world, being turned down by more promising people, until finally making a deal with the poor Hebrews, who need him. "I've got good news and I've got bad news," says Moses, in the corny joke, as he comes down from the Mountain. "The good news is that I managed to talk him down from fifty commandments to only ten. The bad news? One of 'em is still about adultery."

Given the reaction against nature worship, it is perhaps not surprising that the stories of rebellion against the covenant have overtones of returning to the orgiastic rites of a fertility cult. I once saw a production of the Arnold Schoenberg opera *Moses and Aaron,* which was rather graphic about this.

The story of the Golden Calf, the best known of the rebellions, has some overtones of this. Many scholars argue that the young bull, being a common representation of the male sky god in Canaan, is a piece of later propaganda, aimed at the eighth-century northern kingdom of Israel, where an altar of golden bulls was set up under King Jereboam. But it is also true that the Egyptians had their own bull god, Apis. And the real significance of the story is, once again, less historical than theo-political.

The people, we are told in Exodus, chapter 32, are feeling rather insecure, even abandoned. Moses has gone back up the mountain to talk with God about the long delay in entering the Promised Land. They cannot wait. In many ways they are still slaves in mentality. And that, it would appear, is the real significance of the forty years of delay. An entire generation must die off before the Promised Land can be entered. Why? Well, remember: the Israelites did not actually *fight* to escape Pharaoh. All they had to do was leave. And that was hard enough to achieve, since they were so "broken in spirit" that they would not even "hearken unto Moses" (Exod. 6:9). To take over the land of milk and honey from the Canaanites, on the other hand, would require some real, active struggle.

In the Book of Joshua, a full-scale armed conquest of the Promised Land is portrayed. But many scholars today believe that the process was a good deal more gradual than, say, the sun stopping, trumpets blowing, and the walls of Jericho suddenly falling down. It may be, in fact, that the confederation of twelve tribes really arose primarily *in* Palestine; that only a portion of the Israelites had the Exodus experience. Still, the Exodus became the national epic, either through early covenant reaffirmations or, later, through the crisis of the Babylonian exile, or, more likely, in stages. Historically, the so-called "conquest" may simply have been a rural rebellion against Canaanite city-states, vassals to Egypt at the time.

In the Exodus, as in many liberation movements, there is in any case a great ambivalence toward the use of force and violence. Early in the story there is the incident of Moses killing an Egyptian taskmaster, whom he sees beating a Hebrew slave. "And he looked this way and that way, and when he saw that *there was no man,* he slew the Egyptian, and hid him in the sand." The rabbis explained this by saying that he was looking for someone among the Israelites to stand up, intercede, and defend the beaten slave. "Where there is no man," said Rabbi Hillel, "try to be one." Be a mensch.

Later, when Moses finds the people committing idolatry, he is so angry that he smashes the tablets of the law that God has given him. Then he asks, "Who is on the Lord's side? Come to me." And members of his own tribe, the tribe of Levi, come to him. He tells them: "Thus says the Lord, the God of Israel, 'Put your sword by your side, each of you!'" And then three thousand of the idolators are slain. Moses then repents, and offers his own life to God, in atonement for the people's sins.

Political scientist Michael Walzer, in his brilliant book *Exodus and Revolution*, calls Moses' summoning of the Levites "a political act of the first importance." It "creates a subgroup — we might call it a vanguard — whose members anticipate, at least in their own minds, the 'free people' of the future. In fact, they become the magistrates of the future, the priests and bureaucrats. And meanwhile, in the present, they rule by force; they are the enemies of 'graciousness' and gradualism."[1]

When *can* the sword be used? And by whom? Walzer points out that when St. Augustine finally brought himself to defend the persecution of Christian heretics by the Roman state, he justified his new position with an appeal to Exodus 32, saying that when Moses "afflicted the . . . people by severe correction" he was not like Pharaoh, who had been motivated by "lust of power," but rather "inflamed by love." Later, Thomas Aquinas and Hugo Grotius both warned against magistrates falling into error by imitating such severity, though Calvin and his followers often cited the text. Even "meek Moses," a preacher told the House of Commons during the Puritan Revolution, sometimes had to be "a man of blood." And in our own century, Lincoln Steffens found in the Exodus story a complete vindication of Leninist politics, including dictatorship, purges, and terror.

This is one way to read the story. Walzer calls it the "left revolutionary" way. Combine it with enough emphasis on preserving some ethnic or legal status quo and it can become a "right reactionary" interpretation. There are readings of Exodus on the political/religious right in the modern state of Israel today that would fit that pattern. But most readings of Exodus have not appealed to reactionaries at all, but to people who suffer or sympathize with oppression and suffering. Its strongest influence has gone beyond Judaism to Christianity and Marxism, and reemerges in today's Third World theologies of liberation.

Some of these readings are extreme: utopian and messianic. Walzer points out that, in the history of Israel's religion, there is no doubt about it: later messianic hope *does* build on the Exodus story. Everything in Israel's theology does. And secular forms of messianism can be read back into it. But in the story itself, the Promised Land is not some new Eden, or messianic kingdom; it is simply *a better place than Egypt was*. And this provides the soundest way of reading the text, especially in those key areas where politics and one's religious sensibilities interact.

Walzer calls this a "social democratic" reading. It lays considerable emphasis on equality and the inclusive nature of the moral covenant. "The people answered as one: 'Everything that the Lord has spoken we will do'" (Exod. 19:8). Yet it does recognize a place for leadership.

Consider two more episodes preserved in the Book of Numbers about challenges to Moses and to his leadership. In chapter 11, Moses has put the tabernacle of the ark outside the camp and delivers his prophetic judgments and revelations from there. "But there remained two men in the camp . . . Eldad and Medad . . . and they prophesied in the camp. And there ran a young man and told Moses . . . And Joshua . . . said, 'My lord Moses, forbid them.' But Moses said to him, 'Are you jealous for my sake? Would that all the Lord's people were prophets, that the Lord would put his spirit upon them!'" (Num. 11:26–29).

Eldad and Medad are allowed to prophesy. Independent prophecy, in the name of God, remains a permanent (if often a precarious) feature of Israel's religious life. The hope that Moses has in time becomes the prophet Joel's vision of a messianic age: "And it shall come to pass afterward, that I will pour out my spirit upon all flesh; your sons and your daughters shall prophesy, your old men shall dream dreams, your young men shall see visions. Even upon the menservants and maidservants in those days will I pour out my spirit" (Joel 2: 28–29).

The whole nation will be holy — someday. Meanwhile, however, especially after the Golden Calf, it is clear that without the leadership of some who have vision, the people will perish. There are priests and prophets who both claim authority. In an egalitarian community, how can that be justified? This is the question posed in Numbers 16:3 by the rebel Korah: "You take too much upon you," he says to Moses and Aaron, "seeing all the congregation is holy, every one of them . . . Wherefore then lift ye up yourselves above the congregation of the Lord?" (KJV)

Korah, says Walzer, is "the first left oppositionist in the history of radical politics." Moses doesn't reply in the text. But he does something that any leader, after dealing with enough Korahs, can empathize with: he prays that the earth will open up and swallow them! And it does. Or so it says. But then, at the very end of the Book of Numbers, when the census is taken from which the Book derives its name, we again find the names of Dathan and Abiram, "who contended against Moses and Aaron in the company of Korah, when they contended against the LORD, and the earth . . . swallowed them up together with Korah . . . Notwithstanding, the sons of Korah did not die" (Num. 26:9–11).

No indeed they didn't — thank God! For as annoying as they are, such idealists, who want to act as though the millennium has already arrived, are ever with us. They help to keep leaders honest. Yet in a real Exodus community there *are* leaders who keep the vision, so that we are not tempted by shortcuts. But all the Lord's people ideally share their responsibilities: to sing praises; to live out a "priesthood of all believers"; and to strive for one further thing — a "prophethood of all believers."

In such a community, as the theologian who coined that phrase, James Luther Adams, put it, people also think and work together to interpret "the signs of the times" in the light of their faith; to foresee the consequences of human behavior, both individual and institutional, with the intention of making history instead of being pushed around by it.[2]

The task is to remember the enduring lessons of Exodus. Walzer sums them up this way:

✢ wherever you live, it is probably Egypt
✢ there is a better place, a world more fair, full of promise and hope
✢ the way to it is through the wilderness. There is no other way to get from here to there except by the hard way, being tested as we go

Institutions: Judges to Kings, Priests and Early Prophets

One objection often raised in an era of democracy against the theology of the Hebrew Bible is its use of monarchical language for God as "Lord" or "King." Yet it was precisely the egalitarian norms of the covenant that made Hebrew theology initially and normatively opposed to having any human king. Yahweh is the only king of Israel. The book of Judges tells how the story of how it came about that Israel came to be like other nations, with a monarch.

"In those days there was no king in Israel; each man did what was right in his own eyes." So ends the story (Judg. 21:25). The Israelites control only a portion of Palestine (another challenge to the image of a great "conquest" under Joshua). There is no fixed place of worship. The Ark is moved from place to place. They are subjected, more often than not, to oppression by the kings of surrounding peoples. Only when they cry out to God for help is someone raised up to serve as a "judge" over Israel. Six judges get their stories told; six others get brief mention.

These are bloody stories. The fourth judge is a woman, Deborah. During her time the oppression comes from a Canaanite king and his general, Sisera, who takes refuge in the tent of another woman, Jael, and has a tent-peg driven into his temple while he sleeps. This victory is celebrated in "The Song of Deborah" (Judg. 5), a very ancient poem.

Later the Israelites say to Gideon (Judg. 8:22): "Rule over us, you and your son and your grandson also; for you have delivered us out of the hand of Midian." But Gideon replies, "I will not rule over you, and my son will not rule over you; the Lord will rule over you." But eventually he does designate one of his seventy (!) sons as king. A brother and rival declaims "The Parable of the Trees" (Judg. 9):

"The trees once went out to anoint a king over themselves. So they said to the olive tree, 'Reign over us.' The olive tree answered them, 'Shall I stop producing my rich oil . . . ?' Then the trees said to the fig tree, 'You come and reign over us.' But the fig answered . . . 'Shall I stop producing my sweetness and . . . fruit . . . ?' Then the trees said to the vine, 'You come and reign over us.' But the vine said, 'Shall I stop producing my wine . . . ?' So all the trees said to the bramble, 'You come and reign over us.' And the bramble said, 'If in good faith you are anointing me king over you, then come and take refuge in my shade; but if not, let fire come out of the bramble and devour the cedars of Lebanon'" (Judg. 9:8–15).

No useful tree wants to be king, only the bramble. Entangling itself around the other trees, the bramble increases the danger that all will be destroyed by fire. Which is perhaps a metaphor for war and violence.

Certainly the next ruler, Jephthah, is remembered for entangling himself in a terrible vow: if God will give him a military victory over the Ammonites, whoever greets him first back home will be his burnt offering to God. It's his daughter (Judg. 11). Another "text of terror."

The last story in this series ends in tragedy as well. Samson is the son of a woman long barren, who has been told by an angel that she is to bear a deliverer of Israel. He is to be consecrated to God as a "nazarite," vowing to drink no alcohol, eat nothing unclean, and never let a razor touch his hair. His opponents are the Philistines. The story is more complicated than his famous seduction by Delilah. But when she does find out that Samson will lose his superhuman strength if his hair is cut, he is captured, blinded, and chained to the pillars of the Philistine Temple of Dagon in Gaza, where he prays to God for one last burst of strength, pulling down the temple on himself and three thousand Philistines.

Shortly after the September 11, 2001, suicidal terrorist attacks on the United States by Osama bin Laden's network, I saw a production of the late-nineteenth-century French opera *Samson et Dalilah,* by Camille Saint-Saens. All the French sympathy (and best music) was clearly with the Philistines, portrayed as knowing how to enjoy life. Samson, with his avoidance of wine, and the Israelites were portrayed as Middle Eastern puritans. In the end, Samson brought down the temple by toppling two square pillars that looked distressingly like the twin towers of the World Trade Center. As an antidote to this interpretation of Samson as a suicidal terrorist, I recommend the much more sympathetic view of blind Samson in the verse drama *Samson Agonistes,* by John Milton.

The Book of Judges ends with another "text of terror"—the story of a Levite who, to avoid homosexual rape, offers his concubine instead, then kills her, cuts her into twelve pieces, and sends them to the twelve tribes as a testimony against his assailants. The whole book finally seems designed to justify its last sentence: "In those days there was no king in Israel; each man did what was right in his own eyes" (Judg. 21:25).

At this point the Christian ordering of the books of the Bible inserts the Book of Ruth, from the Hebrew *Ketuvim*. It tells how a Moabite woman named Ruth came to marry into a family from Bethlehem. After she was widowed, she told her widowed mother-in-law, Naomi, "Do not press me to leave you. Where you go, I will go; where you dwell, I will dwell; your people shall be my people and your God my God" (Ruth 1:16). Naomi takes Ruth back to Bethlehem. There she gleans in the fields of a rich man named Boaz, who takes her to his bed on the threshing floor and makes her his wife—and a non-Jewish ancestor of a great king, David, who was known to have such an ancestry.

In the Hebrew Bible, however, we go straight to the Book of Samuel for the story of the prophet Samuel and his role in anointing Saul, then David, as king over Israel.

Like Samson, Samuel was dedicated to God by his mother, Hannah, who had been barren. Her song of thanksgiving on discovering her pregnancy, in fact, is the model for the later song of Mary, the mother of Jesus, in Luke's gospel (Cf. the Song of Hannah in 1 Sam. 2:1–10 to the Magnificat in Luke 1:46–55). Samuel is serving with Eli, the priest of the Lord at Shiloh, where the tabernacle has been set up. Eli's own sons are corrupt priests, but Samuel quite literally hears the call of Yahweh: "Samuel! Samuel!"

Twice he thinks it is the priest calling him. Assured that it is not, Samuel says, "Speak, for your servant listens" (1 Sam. 3:10). Samuel becomes not just a priest, but also a prophet of the Lord (one who hears God's voice), and trusted by all Israel.

When the Philistines capture the Ark of the Covenant in battle, Samuel explains that the *kavod*, or glory of God, has been withdrawn from Israel because of its sins. But the Ark also brings a curse on the Philistines. So they send it back, along with a guilt offering. And

Samuel summons all the Israelites to Mizpah and makes them swear to put away all foreign and fertility deities, confess their own sins, and worship Yahweh alone.

By this point Samuel is also a judge over Israel. But the role has become not only one of deciding disputes, but also of providing at least in-termittent military leadership. Other nations have hereditary kings as war leaders. Though warned by Samuel that a king will make demands on them, the people repeatedly insist they want a king like other nations.

A young man named Saul comes to Samuel as to a seer, looking for where to find a lost animal. Samuel anoints him with oil as king, telling the people that just as God once gave them Moses and Aaron, so now God has given them Saul. And just as Moses was both ruler and prophet, Saul then falls into the kind of "prophetic frenzy" out of which the ancient prophets spoke their oracles.[1]

Soon all the people say to Samuel, "Pray to the Lord ... for your servants . . . for we have added to all our other sins the evil of demanding a king for ourselves." When Saul prepares for battle with the Philistines, and Samuel does not come to the camp quickly enough to do the offerings to God, Saul does the sacrifices himself, as though he were also a priest and, like Jephthah, makes a rash curse: death to any soldier who takes food before nightfall on a day of battle. Saul's son Jonathan hasn't heard the order. Having tasted honey from a honeycomb found on the battlefield, he has to be ransomed from death by the people.

Soon Samuel hears the Lord telling him, "I regret that I made Saul king" (1 Sam. 15:11) and to go to the house of Jesse and anoint a king from among his sons. The choice falls on the youngest, David, who is out keeping the sheep. When he is anointed, the spirit of God departs from Saul.

Saul feels tormented by an evil spirit and sends for someone to calm him by playing the lyre. David goes as Saul's servant. And when the Philistines send out their giant, Goliath, to challenge an individual Israelite to battle, it is young David who declines the offer of a sword, or shield, or helmet, and goes out to face him with just a slingshot and five smooth stones from the streambed.

In an essay called "The Five Smooth Stones of Religious Liberalism," liberal theologian James Luther Adams once said that even today religious liberals similarly refuse to go out armed with heavy creeds, doctrines, and confessional statements in confronting the giant evils of the world. Instead, they carry only five well-worn principles of progressive religious living:[2]

1) The conviction that "revelation is not sealed./ Answering now to our endeavor, truth and right are still revealed." Scripture is useful, but never God's final word.

2) Relationships between people should be covenantal; that is, they should rest on mutuality and persuasion as much as possible, not on coercion and power-over.

3) We share a human obligation to work toward what Dr. King called "the Beloved Community" of love and justice.[3]

4) Merely thinking ourselves virtuous and well-intentioned won't get us there. We must forgo notions of the immaculate conception of our own virtue and instead practice the organization of power and the power of organization in order to realize the social incarnation of the good we love.

5) With all the universe provides and with the openness of history, we are never justified in an ultimate pessimism, but must ever keep faith with the future.

Despite his lack of heavy armor and weaponry, David defeats Goliath. Saul gives him his daughter Michal as wife, but then becomes mad with jealousy over David's popularity. Only David's close friendship with Saul's son Jonathan — a love "surpassing the love of women" — protects him. David flees from Saul and forms a guerrilla army. Twice he has a chance to kill Saul, but spares him. Saul seeks the help of a female seer (or "witch") at Endor, but nothing helps. The Philistines defeat Saul, killing him and three of his sons. David mourns for Saul and for Jonathan: "Lo, how the mighty have fallen!" (2 Sam. 1:19 KJV).

But David still has to contend against Saul's army, under the command of General Abner, who has declared Saul's surviving son Ishbaal as king of all Israel. David is anointed king of Judah at Hebron. A long war ensues, but Abner defects and is murdered by David's general, Joab;

Ishbaal is murdered; and the tribes of Israel come to David, accepting him as the shepherd-king of all Israel. He establishes his capital at Jerusalem, capturing the citadel of Zion and building a palace there. When he brings the Ark into the city, he dances before the Lord naked. Michal disapproves, so David has no children by Saul's daughter, only by his many other wives and royal concubines.

The prophet Nathan rebukes David for not building a house for God, who is nonetheless committed to David, saying through the prophet, "I will be a father to him, and he shall be a son to me. When he commits iniquity, I will punish him with a rod such as mortals use, with blows inflicted by human beings. But I will not take my steadfast love from him, as I took it from Saul . . . Your house and your kingdom shall be made sure forever before me." David promises to build a temple (2 Sam. 7). Though only his son Solomon completes the project, God's seemingly unconditional promise to David and his heirs sacralizes the dynasty.

Not that the prophets stop challenging the king for misconduct. Take the salacious story that outdoes Bill Clinton and Monica Lewinsky. David lays eyes on Bathsheba, wife of Uriah the Hittite, bathing on her rooftop, and sends for her to be brought to his bed. She becomes pregnant. So David sends for Uriah, hoping he will go home to her and think he is the father. He's a good officer, however, and refuses to go home to his wife if his soldiers can't do likewise. David has him sent to the front of the battle lines, where he dies. Nathan then comes to tell David the story of a rich man who has stolen a poor man's one little ewe lamb. David declares that the rich man deserves to die. "Thou art the man!" Nathan thunders, declaring that David has done evil in God's sight. David confesses that indeed he has.

It is not that David goes unpunished. The child he has conceived with Bathsheba falls ill. David prays for forgiveness and fasts. But when the child dies, he astonishes his servants by rising and taking food, saying that he knows he cannot bring the child back again. When he consoles Bathsheba, she conceives another son, later named Solomon. David's sin is also later punished when his eldest son, Amnon, replicates his father's sin by raping his half-sister, named Tamar.[4] Her brother Absalom avenges the violation of his sister by killing Amnon and David's other sons. Absalom is banished, but a woman of Tekoa tells him a story that, like Nathan's, provokes self-recognition and repentance. Absalom returns to Jerusalem, though not to his father's presence—but then rebels and tries to usurp the throne for himself. David has to flee Jerusalem, but puts down the rebellion. When he is told that Absalom has been killed, he weeps, saying, "O my son, Absalom, my son, my son Absalom! Would that I had died instead of you, O Absalom, my son, my son!" (2 Sam. 18:33).

There are other rebellions, but David prevails, prospers, and composes songs of thanksgiving (2 Sam. 22). But he also angers God by ordering a census (2 Sam. 24) and raising taxes while leaving the temple still unbuilt. Before he dies his repentance leads him to buy a threshing floor in Jerusalem on which an altar to God is finally raised. When King David is old, a beautiful young woman named Abishag warms his bed but he does not "know her" sexually (1 Kings 1). His son Adonijah tries to organize to succeed him, but Bathsheba goes to David at Nathan's suggestion and gets him to declare her son Solomon his successor.

After his father dies, Solomon prays for wisdom above all things (1 Kings 3) and is granted that and much more. Under Solomon, the Davidic monarchy becomes a small empire. A glorious temple is built, and a new royal palace, using cedars of Lebanon given by King Hiram of Tyre. Solomon dedicates the Temple with a solemn prayer (1 Kings 8). Tributes and visits come from monarchs like the Queen of Sheba. Solomon takes many foreign wives, but in the judgment of the Deuteronomic historian who later edited this court history, he angers God by allowing them all to worship their own gods.

The punishment is that Solomon's son Jeroboam rebels even before his father's death, becoming king over the ten northern tribes of Israel. He establishes a capital at Shechem. In Jerusalem, Solomon's successor as king of the southern kingdom of Judah is another son, Rehoboam. The united kingdom of David is permanently divided.

Both kingdoms are officially Yahwist in religion. The worship of the Canaanite nature deities, Baal and Asherah, however, appeals to people dependent upon the fertility of the land and on the regularity of the rains. In popular religion, Yahweh is sometimes said to have a female consort, an Asherah. There are priests of Yahweh and priests of Baal and

Asherah, not to mention seers who prophesy in their names. Worship takes place at many hilltop shrines.

Yahwist priests claim membership in the tribe of Levi, to which both Moses and Aaron belonged. They have no tribal territory of their own, however, but are scattered throughout the land and given certain rights in many of the cities and towns. Until the building of the temple in Jerusalem, the Ark of the Covenant had been simply housed behind curtains in a tentlike tabernacle. There also seem to have been several lines of Yahwist priesthood, one claiming descent from Moses, another from Aaron. After the building of the temple in Jerusalem, however, the priests there are referred to as "sons of Aaron" and chief priests as "sons of Zadok," David's appointee. They were assisted by other Levites. As the regulations for worship in the Book of Leviticus make clear, the rites of the Temple centered on animal sacrifices—substitutes for human guilt and thanks; offerings for both festival and daily worship. We may be repulsed by ritual sacrifice, but in the ancient world, it was hardly distinctive to the Hebrews.

The temple and its priests, however, did represent an accommodation to the "way of all the earth," just as monarchy did. That left the more distinctive and progressive elements to the prophets.

The Hebrew word for prophet is *nabi'*, "one called," or "sent," as a messenger. Samuel and Nathan are true, reliable messengers of Yahweh. But there are also false prophets. Some prophesy on behalf of other gods or idols, like Baal. There are also those who claim to prophecy on behalf of Yahweh, but corruptly or insincerely. And finally, there are prophets of the Lord who really are sincere, but are simply *wrong* about what God wants or intends, who get proven wrong by the unfolding of history.

Whenever progressive people want to assert that they stand in a "prophetic tradition" by speaking out for justice, some humility is needed. James Luther Adams said that ratio of false prophets to true probably has not changed much since the time of Elijah: 450 to 1.

Elijah lives under King Ahab of the Northern Kingdom. Queen Jezebel is a devotee of Baal. She has all the prophets of Yahweh killed. Elijah alone remains alive and interprets a drought as punishment on the land. His prophetic authority is proven by his ability to perform wonders. When a poor woman gives him hospitality, he restores her son to life and leaves her with jars that are never empty of meal and oil. Then he challenges the 450 prophets of Baal to make it rain. An altar is prepared on Mt. Carmel. They ask Baal to light it. When Elijah prepares at altar to Yahweh, fire does come and the prophets of Baal are killed (1 Kings 18).

Elijah has to flee from Queen Jezebel. Hiding in a cave on Mt. Horeb, God comes to Elijah — but not in the great wind, or in the earthquake, or the fire, but in the "still small voice," or silence that follows (1 Kings 19).

Ahab has coveted poor Naboth's vineyard. Jezebel has the man killed to obtain it. Elijah confronts the king (1 Kings 21). When Ahab earlier had cried out, "Is that you, troubler of Israel?" Elijah had replied, "It is not I who brought trouble on Israel, but you and your father's house, by forsaking the commandments of Yahweh and going after Baalim." Now he simply pronounces defeat, death, and disaster for Ahab. The king gets other prophets to make more positive pronouncements, but he is defeated and killed.

Eventually Elijah passes his prophetic mantle to his disciple, Elisha, and is portrayed as being taken right up into heaven (2 Kings 2). He does not die. This is why later tradition expects Elijah to come again, to usher in the reversal and fulfillment of history in an era marked by the universal reign and worship of God.

Prophecy develops in the Bible as a kind of counterinstitution. Its purpose is to warn rulers, priests, and the complacent among the people about the consequences of breaking covenant with the God of justice, and the likelihood of being judged in history.

One thing that distinguishes prophets from priests is that the prophets have little use for acts of piety per se. They want to see justice being done. As the prophet Amos says on behalf of Yahweh: "I hate, I despise your feast days, and I will not take delight in your solemn assemblies. Though ye offer me burnt offerings . . . I will not accept them . . . Take away from me the noise of thy songs; for I will not hear the melody of thine harps. But let justice run down like waters, and righteousness like a mighty stream" (Amos 5:21–24).

Or as the prophet Micah asks, "With what shall I come before the

Lord, and bow myself before God on high? Shall I come before him with burnt offerings? . . . Will the Lord be pleased with thousands of rams? Shall I give my firstborn for my transgression, a fruit of my body for the sin of my soul? He has shown you, O man, what is good; and what does the Lord require of you, but to do justice, and to love mercy, and to walk humbly with thy God?" (Micah 6:6–8).

Prophetic oracles such as these were not simply preserved for their high spirituality and literary qualities, though they surely had those. As a whole, the warnings of the prophets who gave them had also been vindicated by history. They had seen correctly the coming fall of Israel, which came in 722 B.C.E., and the subsequent destruction of Jerusalem and Judah, in 587 B.C.E., and the Exile in Babylon. Not in every detail, perhaps. The prophet Jeremiah is forced to complain, "O Lord, thou hast deceived me . . ." (20:7 KJV) and Isaiah to admit, "For my thoughts are not your thoughts, neither are your ways my ways, saith the Lord" (Isa. 55:8 KJV).

We will examine the "literary" prophets like these, whose words were preserved for us in entire collections, in a subsequent chapter. Here suffice it to say that the prophets who were remembered, as opposed to those prophets whose names or oracles were forgotten, read the signs of the times with some accuracy.

Today, when we may ask who is performing the role of the prophet, no one vocation entirely fills the role. It is not just social activists, journalists, environmentalists, scientists, or other courageous leaders who really do warn us about the dangers of ignoring the consequences of our actions. It is also the artist, since what the prophet does is to paint pictures with words, showing an alternative view of reality, one seen from an angle that the powerful and the pious do not always want to see.

True prophets are never called to be tolerant of evil. But what is striking about the Bible is that so many of their condemnations were not only tolerated by those who heard them but preserved as authoritative by those who assembled the sacred writings of the people. At the time, says Abraham Joshua Heschel, "to patriots, they must have seemed pernicious; to the pious, blasphemous; to the authorities, seditious." They often attacked reliance on military might, or alliances, cultic worship, or worldly wisdom. They dared to interpret the enemies of Israel as instruments of God, speaking of "Assyria, the rod of my anger" (Isaiah) and "Nebuchadnezzar, the King of Babylon, My servant" whom I will bring "against this land and its inhabitants" (Jer. 25:9).

Like people in our time, the ancient Israelites wanted to hear that their enemies were evil and despised by God. Their values were commonly the values of the world at large, which always values things like wisdom, wealth, and might. They wanted to rely only on these things and on themselves. But prophets arose among them who dared to denigrate such an approach: "The wisdom of their wise shall perish," says Isaiah (29:14). "Ah, but I am rich, I have gained wealth for myself," Hosea hears Ephraim/Israel say. "But all his riches can never offset/ The guilt he has incurred" (12:8). And as for might: "Because you have trusted in your chariots/ And in the multitude of your warriors,/ Therefore the tumult of war shall arise among your people,/ And all your fortresses shall be destroyed" (Hos. 10:13–14).

"Thus sayeth the Lord: 'Let not the wise man glory in his wisdom, let not the mighty man glory in his might, let not the rich man glory in his riches. But let him who glories, glory in this: that he understands and knows Me — that I am the Lord who practices kindness, justice, and righteousness on earth; for in these I delight,' says the Lord" (Jer. 9:23–24 KJV).

The prophet's most characteristic tone may be one of warning, but the prophetic vocation is not primarily about prediction or about the future. It is about interpreting the present; reading signs of the times and showing consequences from a God's-eye point of view. False prophets may take a narrower point of view, speaking out of more tribal and local pieties. The very definition of idolatry, as we have said, is substituting the partial for the whole. The culture may practice patriarchal partiality, the Yahwist priesthood may be all male, but God does inspire women such as Huldah also to be prophets in Israel (2 Kings 22:14; 2 Chron. 34:22).

The prophetic reality is always a relational reality: "Hear this word that the Lord has spoken against you, O people of Israel, against the whole family which I brought up out of the land of Egypt. You only have I known of all the families of the earth; therefore I will punish you for all your iniquities" (Amos 3:1–2).

Within the relational realities of history, things are not already fated. The call is for *teshuvah,* for turning or returning to the covenant in which Yahweh's justice and compassion, God's *hesed* or steadfast love, is ever present. Evildoers and those leaning on false sources of spiritual security are never considered beyond redemption.

Exaltations: The Book of Psalms

If the prophets' words are a series of condemnations, decrying those who would rely upon what is not whole or holy, then the hymnbook of the Bible takes a different approach to trying to restore the covenant between God and God's people, through exaltations designed to re-enthrone Yahweh "on the praises of Israel."

Perhaps, however, one cannot be understood apart from the other. For just as liberation cannot be understood apart from oppression, exaltation of God cannot be understood apart from lamentation over injustice, despair, bitterness, moral confusion, and even the desire from vindication and revenge. One of the strengths of the Bible, and of the Psalms, is that they both encompass the full range of human emotions—yet within a framework of ultimate praise. Just as God pronounced the creation good so for human beings, "It is a good thing . . . to sing praises" (Ps. 92: 1).

In Hebrew, the collection we know as Psalms is called *Sefer tehillim,* "the Book of Praises." It's related to the word *hallel,* which means "praise," and the collection includes a whole group known by that name (Pss. 113–118). The book's final word is "hallelujah," meaning "Praise ye the Lord." Yet the simpler word, "psalm," from the Greek word for a poem set to music, may be even more descriptive. For the 150 hymns in this "hymnbook of the Second Temple" range from brief lyrics through laments, prayers, didactic meditations, to elaborate recitations of individual and collective experiences.

As a whole, they are traditionally attributed to the "sweet singer of Israel," David the King, who as a youth sang soothing songs to Saul while playing the lyre. Some carry superscriptions associating them with particular events in the life of David. Psalm 57 is headed, "when he fled from Saul, in the cave." Psalm 18, "when the Lord delivered him from the hand of Saul," is also found in the narrative history at 2 Samuel 22:2–51. Psalm 51, a great expression of remorse and contrition, is headed "when Nathan the prophet came unto him after he had gone into Bathsheba." Psalm 3, which begins, "O Lord, how many are my foes!" is called, "A Psalm of David, when he fled from Absalom his son." Psalm 72, which concludes with the words "The prayers of David, the son of Jesse, are ended," constitutes an ethical will, directed to his son and successor, and therefore is called a Psalm of Solomon.

But the heading, *le'Dawid*, like *le'Solomon*, need not mean *by* David. It can also mean "concerning," or "for," or "in the style of." All together, seventy-three of the psalms carry this designation. Structurally, the Psalter seems, like any hymnal, to have been largely assembled out of earlier collections. Some give new words to be sung to familiar tunes, like Psalm 22, to be sung "according to The Hind of the Dawn."

Fragments of hymns, especially songs of exaltation, constitute some of the oldest materials we have in the Bible. The Song of Miriam and the Song of the Sea, in Exodus 15, are examples already mentioned. Even the Creation story, in Genesis 1, may be read as a hymn. For Hebrew poetry doesn't use rhyme, or strict meter, but rather a "rhythm of sense," with heavy reliance on parallel structures. This is especially true in expressions, like the Psalms, chosen or developed for use in worship. There the parallelisms often lent themselves to antiphonal chanting.

The editor has chosen two opening hymns, with themes important in the Second Commonwealth, after the Exile: meditation upon the law, and salvation from tumult among the nations by God's anointed king. Then come:

1. an original Davidic collection (Pss. 3–41)
2. the Psalms of the Korah musical guild (Pss. 42–49)
3. a second Davidic collection (Pss. 51–72)
4. Psalms of the Asaph musical guild (Pss. 73–83, 50)

These last three groups are often called the "Elohistic Psalter," and probably circulated together, as an earlier hymnal, using that term for God. That would explain why Psalm 53 repeats Psalm 14, addressed to Yahweh. Then come:

5. additional psalms of musical guilds (Pss. 84–89)
6. various other collections (Pss. 90–150), including

   a.   Psalms of Yahweh's kingship (Pss. 93–99)
   b.   Psalms of pilgrimage (Pss. 120–134)
   c.   Hallelujah psalms (Pss. 104–106, 111–113, 135, 146–50)

Taken together, the Psalms constitute the longest book in the Bible. They are also, of course, among its most familiar and beloved expressions. In Christian monastic practice, the whole Psalter was to be sung through in community worship once each week. In the daily worship of the Anglican prayer book, the cycle is completed once each month. In the synagogue and many Protestant churches, Sabbath worship will use all the psalms in the course of a year. In the Second Temple, the Psalter was early divided into five "books," each closing with a brief doxology.[1] This fivefold division was meant, no doubt, to mirror the Torah, and to parallel its reading.

This systematic use of the Psalms in worship over the millennia has had a profound influence. The need for exaltation is very human. For what is the alternative? Despair? Cynicism? And so the familiar phrases and praises of the Psalms, perhaps more than any other part of the Bible, have helped to shape the language and culture of the West. Yet for many people, that has become a part of the problem. Familiarity breeds contempt, and they begin by asking, "Who is this God? And why should I offer praise?" One liberal minister once summarized the problem by opening a service with the following words:

> Praise the Lord! Why? He requires it? How insecure, how gluttonous for praise! The Lord wasn't always singing praises; seldom, in fact. More often he was angry, or revengeful, jealous, making deals.
>
> We'll praise what merits praise. What doesn't needs a closer look, in case some cursing is required, for God's sake.[2]

Yet the Psalms don't deny our need to curse, or imply that it is always easy to praise, or say that it's something God requires. On the contrary, I think of Psalm 137. It begins beautifully, poignantly:

> By the rivers of Babylon —
> there we sat down and there we wept

when we remembered Zion.
On the willow there we hung up our harps.
For there our captors asked of us songs,
and our tormentors asked for mirth, saying,
"Sing us one of the songs of Zion."
How shall we sing the Lord's song
in a foreign land?

And it ends with a terrible curse:

Remember, O Lord, against the Edomites
the day of Jerusalem's fall,
how they said, "Tear it down, tear it down!
Down to its foundations!"
O daughter Babylon, you devastator!
Happy shall they be who pay you back
what you have done to us!
Happy shall they be who take your little ones
and dash them against the rock!

The emotion here is starkly realistic as the psalmist remembers
cruelty and desires vengeance. Yet far more often in the Psalms the
emotional shift is in the other direction. The psalmist starts out
feeling threatened, frightened, or worse, cursing his fate and his enemies. Then, between one line and the next, something shifts — toward
faith rather than fear, toward blessing God rather than cursing one's
enemies.

It is a good thing to make this shift, and to sing praises to God, not
because the character of God requires it, but because ours does. It is in
our nature to worship and praise. As Emerson once put it, a human being will worship something, be assured of that. In the Psalms we encounter a very human, very personal voice, speaking on behalf of all of
us, in the first person. Sometimes it curses, yes; so do we. Sometimes it
pleads; so do we. Sometimes it feels abandoned, but it struggles to reject despair, vengeance, and wickedness.

"Create in me a clean heart, O God," it prays, "and put a new and
right spirit within me. Do not cast me away from your presence, and

take not your holy spirit from me. Restore to me the joy of your salvation, and sustain in me a willing spirit" (Ps. 51:10–12).

> As a deer longs for flowing streams,
> so longs my soul for you, O God.
> My soul thirsts for God,
> for the living God.
> When shall I come and behold
> the face of God?
> My tears have been my food day and night,
> while people say to me continually,
> "Where is your God?"
> These things I remember,
> as I pour out my soul:
> how I went with the throng
> and led them in procession
> to the house of God,
> with glad shouts and songs of thanksgiving,
> a multitude keeping festival.
> Why are you cast down, O my soul,
> and why are you disquieted within me?
> Hope in God; for I shall again praise him,
> my help and my God. (Ps. 42:1–5)

Apart from all theological questions, there is an existential truth in the notion that it is a good thing to sing praises. A brief poem by Rainier Maria Rilke perhaps makes the most powerful modern commentary I know on that theme. In translation it reads:[3]

> O tell us, poet, what do you do?—I praise.
> But those dark, deadly, devastating ways,
> how do you bear them, suffer them?—I praise.
> And then the Nameless, beyond guess or gaze,
> how do you call it, conjure it?—I praise.
> And whence your right, in every kind of maze,
> in every mask, to remain true?—I praise.
> And that the mildest and the wildest ways
> know you like star and storm?—Because,
>   I praise.

In a deep sense, the poetry of the Psalms reminds us that we are all priests and poets. We choose to bless or curse. Our perceptions shape us, and often tempt us. ". . . I was envious of the arrogant; I saw the prosperity of the wicked," says the psalmist, describing them (Ps. 73:3–9):

> For they have no pain;
> their bodies are sound and sleek.
> They are not in trouble as others are;
> they are not plagued like other people.
> Therefore pride is their necklace;
> violence covers them as a garment.
> Their eyes swell out with fatness,
> their hearts scoff and speak with malice;
> They set their mouths against the heavens,
>> and their tongues range over the earth.

They say, "How can God know? Is there knowledge in the Most High?" (Ps. 73:11). But the psalmist affirms being known and encompassed by the one Creator of all things, who is also a kind of poet, having made all nature a message:

> The heavens are telling the glory of God;
> and the firmament proclaims his handiwork.
> Day to day pours forth speech,
> and night to night declares knowledge.
> There is no speech, nor are there words;
> their voice is not heard;
> yet their voice goes out through all the earth,
> and their words to the end of the earth.
> In the heavens he has set a tent for the sun,
> which out like a bridegroom
>> from his wedding canopy, and
>> like a strong man runs its course with joy.
> Its rising is from the end of the heavens,
> and its circuit to the end of them;
> and there is nothing hid from its heat.

This is the first part of Psalm 19, which has been combined with another song, as though to make the connection between what we would call natural and moral law:

> The law of the Lord is perfect,
>   reviving the soul;
> the decrees of the Lord are sure,
>   making wise the simple;
> the precepts of the Lord are right,
> rejoicing the heart;
> the commandment of the Lord is clear,
> enlightening the eyes;
> the fear of the Lord is pure, enduring for ever.

The *Idea of the Holy*, as Rudolph Otto pointed out in his classic book of that title, connects the awesome beauty of creation with the tremendous sense that our moral lives are finite and will be judged in time. A wise spiritual guide among my elders says that when he wakes up in the middle of the night, unable to sleep and fretting, what often calms him are the words of the 139th Psalm, one of the most beloved:

> O Lord, you have searched me and known me
> You know when I sit down and when I rise up;
> You discern my thoughts from far away.
> You search out my path and my lying down,
> and are acquainted with all my ways.
> Even before a word is on my tongue,
> O Lord, you know it completely.
> You hem me in, behind and before,
> and lay your hand upon me.
> Such knowledge is too wonderful for me;
> it is so high that I cannot attain it.
> Where can I go from thy spirit?
> or whither shall I flee from your presence?
> If I ascend up to heaven, you art there;
> If I make my bed in Sheol, you are there.
> If I take the wings of the morning
> and settle at the farthest limits of the sea,
> even there your hand shall lead me,

> and your right hand shall hold me fast.
> If I say, "Surely the darkness shall cover me:
> even the light around me become night,"
> even the darkness is not dark to you;
> the night is as bright as the day,
> for darkness is as light to you.
> For it was you who formed my inward parts;
> You knit me together in my mother's womb.
> I will praise you,
> for I am fearfully and wonderfully made:
> Wonderful are your works; that I know very well.

Speaking of making one's bed in Sheol, that word is sometimes translated as "hell." But the ancient Hebrews had no real concept of a place of punishment beyond this life. Sheol is simply the place of no return, the grave.

The Psalms are utterly realistic about death. For that reason alone, they have long had an important role in dealing with grief. I myself have never been able to conduct a memorial service or a funeral for someone I felt close to without either including or finding myself praying at least one psalm. Not that there is some doctrine of immortality that is affirmed there. There isn't.

"I will praise the Lord while I live," says one psalm (146:2), and another, "The dead do not praise the Lord, nor do any that go down into silence" (115:17). As we have noted, the spirituality of Israel was shaped in stark contrast to the obsession with immortality that characterized Egyptian religion. It is not death that is feared, but grief that is real. Of all the psalms, surely the one that is best known is the twenty-third. In its traditional translation it reads:

> Yea though I walk through the valley
> of the shadow of death, I will fear no evil;
> for thou art with me; thy rod and thy staff,
>   they comfort me.
> Thou preparest a table before me
>   in the presence of mine enemies;
> thou anointest my head with oil; my cup
>   overfloweth.

Surely goodness and mercy shall follow me
all the days of my life;
and I shall dwell in the house of the Lord forever.

Or, more accurately, "for as long as I live." There is no implication of
eternity at the end. The phrase is *le orekh yomim,* "for length of days."
What the psalmist is saying is just simply, "I shall be wrapped up in this
grace of Yours for the whole of my life."[4]

But a word about translations. Often the best way to understand a
given Psalm is to read it in several modern translations. As I mentioned
before, there are familiar phrases from the King James version, like
the one about worshiping the Lord "in the beauty of holiness," (Pss.
29:6; 96:9) which have the character of "beloved mistranslations." That
phrase, sadly, turns out to refer not to a spirit of humility, but to the
"holy splendor" (NRSV), either of God's glory or of priestly garments
used in worship.

All poetry is notoriously difficult to translate. What is remarkable
about the Psalms is that, across such distances in time and space, they
come down to us with such continuing spiritual power. Some of that
power is rooted in the sheer concreteness and physicality of the language. Take the word "spirit," for example. In Hebrew, the word *ruach*
means not only that but "breath" and "wind." It is very physical, as in
the name Rachel, *Ruach-el,* "the breath of God."

The poetry of the Psalms is similarly physical and active, not
abstract. The mountains "skip like rams" (114:6). The way in which
the psalmist is spiritually uplifted by the thought of God's covenant
is conveyed by the image of wings: "Hide me in the shadow of your
wings . . ." (17:8), and "in the shadow of your wings I sing for joy"
(63:8). Those who meditate upon God's law are said to be "like trees
planted by streams of water, which yield their fruit in its season, and
their leaves do not wither" (1:2–3; cf. 92:13). At other times, God is referred to as having the firm solidity of a rock, or a fortress (19:15;
144:1–2; 46; etc.).

Even the word "heart" is used very concretely. The word in Hebrew
is *lev,* and means the physical organ. "Test my heart and my reins," my
kidneys, says Psalm 26:2 in the KJV; the NRSV reads "mind." "You

have put gladness in my heart," says another Psalm (4:7). Others refer to "the upright in heart" (7:10) as opposed to those who speak "with a double heart" (12:2), or, literally, "with a heart and a heart." "The Lord is near to the brokenhearted" (34:18). A "broken and contrite heart" God will not despise (51:17). It is in his heart that the fool says "There is no God" (14:1), while the psalmist's prayer is, "Let the words of my mouth and the meditation of my heart be acceptable to you, O Lord, my rock and my redeemer" (19:15).

Even when the Psalms give what might be called creedal affirmations, what they recite are the concrete deeds in history attributed to God—especially the redemption from Egypt, as in the so-called "historical Psalms," like 136, but also Creation, as in Psalm 24 (KJV):

> The earth is the Lord's and the fullness thereof,
>   the world and those who dwell therein;
> for he has founded it upon the seas,
>   and established it upon the rivers.
> Who shall ascend the hill of the Lord?
>   And who shall stand in his holy place?
> He who has clean hands and a pure heart,
>   who does not lift up his soul to what is false,
>   and does not swear deceitfully.
> He will receive blessing from the Lord,
>   and vindication from the God of his salvation,
> Such is the generation of those who seek him,
>   who seek the face of the God of Jacob.
> Lift up your heads, O ye gates!
>   and be lifted up, O ancient doors!
>   that the King of glory may come in.
> Who is this King of glory?
>   The Lord, strong and mighty,
>   the Lord, mighty in battle!
> Lift up your heads, O ye gates!
>   and be lifted up, O ancient doors!
>   that the King of glory may come in.
> Who is this king of glory!
>   The Lord of hosts, he is the King of glory!

As such a psalm indicates, even in the days of the monarchy, the theological norm was that Yahweh was the true king of the land, just as it was with the prophets. For now, we can conclude by saying that while frustration is far from a minor theme in the Bible, exaltation is what we remember. It is a good thing to sing praises. Hallelujah! Amen.

Frustrations: The Wisdom Literature and Job

There is a body of literature in the Hebrew Bible that stands apart. It is often referred to as "wisdom literature" and has little to do with Israel's distinctive sacred history or the prophets' call for return to the covenant. It borrows from the scribal and wisdom traditions throughout the ancient Near East. Because of that, it can seem more universal, experiential, philosophical, and practical. All these things have a certain appeal for us. Books like Ecclesiastes and Proverbs fit here. Because it raises the philosophical question of God's justice, and is based on an old Near Eastern folktale, so does the Book of Job. No biblical story has more engaged modern wrestling with God and with the question of Why Bad Things Happen to Good People, as in the well-known book of that title by Rabbi Harold Kushner.

PROVERBS

The oldest of this wisdom literature is contained in the Book of Proverbs. Like the Psalms, this sprawling collection of wise sayings and poems did not receive its final literary frame until rather late, after the Exile. Just as Psalms is attributed to David, Proverbs is attributed to his son Solomon the wise, at whose court, in Israel's golden age, the tenth century B.C.E., "wisdom teachers" from abroad may have first set up shop among the Hebrews. Embedded in the middle of Proverbs (22:17–24, 34) is a collection of sayings heavily dependent on an Egyptian text, "The Instruction of Amen-em-ope," which may be older than 1000 B.C.E.

The surrounding chapters (10–29) seem to collect sayings from the four centuries before the Exile. The wit and parallelism of the original Hebrew is hard to convey, especially when the familiar phrasings of the King James translation have become so, well, *proverbial:*

"Where there is no vision, the people perish" (29:18).
"A good name is to be chosen rather than great riches" (22:1).
"Pride goeth before destruction, and a haughty spirit
before a fall" (16:8).
"A soft answer turneth away wrath: but grievous words
stirreth up anger" (15:1).
"Wine is a mocker, strong drink is raging: whosoever is deceived
thereby is not wise" (20:10).
"Treasures of wickedness profit nothing: but righteousness
delivereth from death" (10:2).

This is wisdom given to affirming a sense of social order, promising rewards in this life for good behavior and dire consequence for bad, and full of spiritual advice of the practical kind, for the frustrations of dealing with temptations, evil companions, fools, and the self-deluded. It also contains some notoriously problematic advice about child rearing: "He who spares the rod hates his son, but he who loves him disciplines him early ..." "Do not withhold discipline from a child; if you beat him with a rod he will not die. Beat him with a rod and you will save him from the grave" (13:24; 23:13–14 NRSV).

We all need discipline, adults and children alike, but this turns enduring wisdom about parenting inside out—as though parents who are self-disciplined enough to restrain an impulse to strike a child are unloving while those who are physically abusive are kind! The patriarchal aspect of the morality in Proverbs is apparent in many of its attitudes toward family. The book culminates, for example, in an ode to a capable wife:

"A capable wife who can find? She is far more precious than jewels. The heart of her husband trusts in her and he will have no lack of gain ... She rises while it is still night and provides food for her household and tasks for her servant-girls ... Her husband is known in the city gates, taking his seat among the elders of the land ... She looks well to the ways of her household, and does not eat the bread of idleness" (31:10, 15, 23, 27). Note that it is her household, and not his, yet as in all patriarchy, the realm of woman is that of necessity, while men occupy the realm of freedom and political determination.

A more egalitarian, feminist interpretation of Wisdom, however, appears in the first nine chapters of Proverbs. Here Wisdom is portrayed as a woman crying in the streets, like a prophetess. Although she is juxtaposed with the temptations of prostitutes and of personified Folly, also female, this feminine Wisdom (in Hebrew, *hokhmah*; and in Greek, *sophia*) was often understood as eternal, as having been with God from the very beginning.

In later Judaism, *Hokhmah* became understood as a female aspect or emanation of the Divine, identified with the whole instruction of the Torah, both written and oral.[1] In early Christianity, Holy Wisdom, or *hagia sophia* in Greek, was not only the name of the great church built by the emperor Constantine in his capital, it was also seen as a feminine aspect of the Logos, the Word made flesh.

The notion of Wisdom as eternal with God and as active in the world on God's behalf was commonplace by the time of Jesus. "Wisdom," he said, "is justified by all her children" (Luke 7:35). "Wisdom was created before all things," says the Wisdom of Jesus ben Sirach, also known as Ecclesiasticus (1:4). The Wisdom of Solomon, written in Greek, calls Sophia "an initiate in the knowledge of God and an associate in his works" (8:4). Feminist biblical interpretation justifiably sees this once strong tradition of Divine Wisdom as having been pushed aside in the process of transmission by patriarchal forces protecting male privilege.[2]

I remember sitting next to a male colleague at a gathering where a particularly fiery religious feminist was denouncing the many evils of patriarchal society in ardent terms. My friend muttered aloud, "Sometimes I think the wrath of the Mother God makes the wrath of the Father God look mild!" Behind us was a young woman minister who, overhearing, leaned forward, put her hands on both our shoulders, and said, "Yes, gentlemen, and in the fear of God is the beginning of wisdom!"

"The fear of the Lord is the beginning of *knowledge*," says Proverbs 1:7, "fools despise wisdom and instruction." While the consequences of our foolish behavior are surely one reason to have "fear" of God, the word in English lacks the tone of awe and humility implied in the Hebrew. Proverbs 8:13–14 explains the phrase simply in behavioral terms:

"The fear of the Lord is hatred of evil. Pride and arrogance, and the way of evil, and the perverse speech do I hate," Wisdom says. "I have counsel and sound wisdom. I have insight, I have strength."

ECCLESIASTES

A much more jaded view of wisdom, but one we can easily identify with, is to be found in the book of Ecclesiastes: "For in much wisdom is much vexation, and those who increase knowledge increase sorrow" (1:18). This is the kind of proverbial wisdom that seems to suffer from skepticism even about its own value. At times it sounds like so much spiritual fatigue: "Vanity of vanities, all is vanity, saith the Preacher," the King James version begins (1:2). These are announced as "the words of the Qoheleth, the son of David, king in Jerusalem" (1:1). It is an odd term, a feminine participle related to the root word meaning to assemble — the person who addresses the assembly, translated into Greek as Ecclesiastes.

Hebrew scholars point out that the word translated as "vanity" really means "vapor" or "breath" in the original. The words even sound like breathing: "*Havel havaleem, ha-kol havel.*" "Breath of breaths, everything is breath." The author recounts his own experience: "I said to myself, 'Come, I will plunge into pleasures and enjoy myself'; but this too was emptiness . . . I undertook great works; I built myself houses and planted vineyards. . . . Then I turned and reviewed all my handiwork, all my labour and toil, and I saw that everything was emptiness and chasing the wind, of no profit under the sun . . . I set myself to look at wisdom and at madness and folly . . . [but] Who knows whether he will be a wise man or a fool? . . . This too is emptiness" (2:1–19, in part, NEB).

"Then I turned and gave myself up to despair . . . There is nothing better for a man to do than to eat and drink and enjoy himself in return for his labours. And yet I saw that this too comes from the hand of God. For without him who can enjoy his food, or who can be anxious? God gives wisdom and knowledge and joy to the man who pleases him, while to the sinner he gives the trouble of gathering and amassing wealth only to hand it over to someone else who pleases God. This too is emptiness and chasing the wind" (Eccles. 2:1–26 NEB). In chapter 3, we find the famous passage that begins, "To everything there is a season, and a time for every purpose under heaven." Perhaps it's not too much to say that in Ecclesiastes what we find is a kind of religious existentialism. Unconvinced that the ways of God can ever be fully understood, the emphasis is on human choice and gratitude. Life is brief, too precious to waste. We are but breaths of a larger breath not our own. The difficult thing is to do the right thing at the right time. We can either pursue ephemeral, fleeting things, or we can choose to breathe deeply, live fully, savor life, and love one another while we have time, sanctifying each moment and every breath we take by the quality of our living.

The focus here is on accepting one's portion (*heleq*) or lot in life. There is no Wisdom with a capital W now—no mediation between the frustrating cycles of human existence and the timeless realm of God. The author writes, "Go thy way, eat thy bread with joy, and drink thy wine with a merry heart. . . . Whatever thy hand finds to do, do it with thy might . . . Truly the light is sweet, and a pleasant thing it is to behold the sun . . . So behold the sun before the dust returns to earth and thy spirit goes back to the God who gave it in thy final breath. Breath of breath . . . everything is breath" (Eccles. 9:7,10;11:7; 12:7–8 NEB).

SONG OF SONGS

And now we come to the heavy breathing!

How a collection of erotic love poetry came to be included in the Bible might perhaps best be attributed to the influence of Wisdom. Certainly the lowercase wisdom of the rabbis and church fathers was sorely tested by it. The rabbis accepted it only because, once again, these poems were attributed to Solomon. Since Solomon was said to have had seven hundred wives and three hundred concubines, this had some logic, but the collection clearly took its literary form much later, though some verses are as old as Solomon, for all we know.

More importantly, the prophets had often spoken of the relationship between Yahweh and Israel using the metaphor of marriage. In thor-

oughly sexist ways, mind you: often comparing the people to an unfaithful wife "whoring after foreign gods." Letting his foreign wives
worship gods and goddesses of their own was, in fact, one of the criti-
cisms of Solomon in the Deuteronomic history. The church fathers
were even more uncomfortable with the frankly sensual, sexual character of these poems, but accepted them under an allegorical extension
of that interpretation: as "symbolizing the love between Christ and His
Church." Please.

When Bishop John S. Spong wrote his book, *Rescuing the Bible from
Fundamentalism,* he began with a preamble entitled, "Sex Drove Me
to the Bible!"[3] I know what he means. Another religious writer, Frederick Buechner, puts it this way, "Contrary to Mrs. Grundy, sex is not sin;
contrary to Hugh Hefner, sex is not salvation either."[4] The Song of
Songs is the Bible's response to Mrs. Grundy (Hugh gets his elsewhere):

> "O that his left hand were under my head, and his right hand
> embraced me!" (2:6; 8:3).
> "My beloved is like a gazelle, or a young stag" (2:9).
> "You are stately as a palm tree and your breasts are
> like its clusters. I say I will climb the palm tree and lay hold
> of its branches" (7:7–8).

Much of the Song is a dialogue between Lover and Beloved (2:10–12):

> My beloved speaks and says to me:
> "Arise my love, my fair one, and come away;
> For lo, the winter is past, the rain is over and gone.
> The flowers appear on the earth,
> the time of singing has come,
> And the voice of the turtledove is heard in our land."

Genre issues concerning the Song of Songs are highly debated. Some
read it as a single, carefully crafted construction; others, as a series of
six or more poems. Whether it was originally a collection of secular love
poetry, or wedding songs, or a sacred marriage liturgy akin to the rit-
uals of marriage between ancient Near Eastern kings, representing a
fertility god like Tammuz, and a priestess representing his divine sis-
ter/consort, Inanna or Astarte, is also not clear. Some recent readings

have even identified the social setting with lovemaking at funeral rites, affirming life by setting the power of love over against the power of death: "Set me as a seal upon your heart, as a seal upon your arm; for love is as strong as death, jealousy is cruel as the grave. Its flashes are flashes of fire, a most vehement flame. Many waters cannot quench love, neither can floods drown it" (8:6–7).

Nor can even the whirlwind carry it away.

JOB

The Book of Job is one of the most intriguing and complex works in the Hebrew Bible. Intriguing, because the issues Job raises — about justice, God, suffering, the gulf between human understanding and the divine order of things — continue to be powerful themes down to our own time. Job provoked twentieth–century humanistic responses as diverse as Archibald MacLeish's play *J.B.,* Carl Jung's *The Answer to Job,* and Robert Frost's verse-drama *The Masque of Reason.* Job is complex, not only because of these themes, but because in the very structure of the Hebrew work as we have it there are tensions.

Take the tension between the "patient" Job and the impatient Job. The first is a proverbial figure. But the bulk of the book is about the second. "The patience of Job" is referred to in the New Testament (cf. James 5:11). The folktale goes back, however, to ancient Mesopotamia, where the deities were often depicted as acting on impulse to test human beings in ways that defy our comprehension. A stark form of this story is found in the prose framework of the Book of Job, its prologue and epilogue (Job 1–2; 42:7–17).

This Job is a devout, righteous man. He is not said to be a Jew, however, or as even given any very concrete or historical setting. In fact, Job is said to dwell "in the land of Oz." In the court of heaven, God mentions him to the Prosecutor (the "Satan"), who declares that it's easy for Job to be devout; he is also prosperous. But take away his goods and he'll curse God. So God gives permission for the test. Job's herds die; his children are killed. Still he says, "Naked I came from my mother's womb, and naked shall I return; the Lord gave, and the Lord has taken away; blessed be the name of the Lord" (1:21 KJV).

Finally, he is afflicted with loathsome sores all over his body and left sitting on an ash heap. Even his wife advises him to "curse God and die." But Job replies, "Shall we receive good at the hand of God, and shall we not receive evil?" (2:9–10). Then three friends come to condole with him and comfort him. They see that his suffering is so great that at first they don't dare speak, just weep and rend their garments with him. In the epilogue, what the friends finally do say is rebuked. Then the patient loyalty of Job is rewarded with new herds, and a new family, more fair and prosperous than he had before.

But in between we hear the impatient Job, not in prose, but in poetic dialogue: first with the three friends, then with a fourth named Elihu, and finally with God, who answers him "out of the whirlwind." This Job begins by doing what his wife has suggested: not dying, but cursing the very day he was ever born. Each of the friends in turn tells him, in essence, that this is no way to behave. Their piety is orthodox. If you suffer, they say, bow to the chastening. God rewards the righteous and punishes the wicked. If Job is suffering, it must be for a reason. He should examine his conscience.

In MacLeish's modern version, *J.B.*, the three comforters are also modern. Only one is a shopworn representative of religious orthodoxy. Of the other two, one is a psycho-reductionist, implying, "You must have brought this on yourself unconsciously." The third is a soap-box social commentator, a quasi-Marxist and historicist who suggests that J.B. must not have read correctly the historical necessities in his situation.

But the original Job doesn't buy any such accusations. "I will hold fast to my righteousness," he tells them, "My heart does not reproach me." Instead, he wants to put God on trial. He wants to know the *why* of his suffering. On this theme, Robert Frost has Job's wife (whom he calls Sarah) say

> Of course, in the abstract high singular
> There isn't any universal reason;
> And no one but a man would think there was.
> You don't catch women trying to be Plato.

In the Hebrew text, a similar point of view enters the dialogue when the three false comforters are talked out, but before Job gets any satisfaction. It comes from a character named Elihu, in chapters 32 through 37. This may be a late interpolation. But it warns human beings against becoming "wise in their own conceit," and emphasizes the enormous gap between human understanding and God's ways. Another interpolation may be in chapter 28, where Job himself is made to say similar things:

> But where shall wisdom be found?
> And where is the place of understanding?
> Man does not know the way to it,
> and it is not found in the land of the living . . .
> God understands the way to it,
>   and he knows its place.
> For he looks to the ends of the earth,
>   and sees everything under the heavens. (28:12–13; 23–24)

In any case, it is God who puts the point most strongly:

> Then the Lord answered Job out of the whirlwind:
> "Who is this that darkens counsel
>   by words without knowledge?
> Gird up your loins like a man,
>   I will question you, and you shall declare to me.
> Where were you when I laid the foundation of the earth?
>   Tell me, if you have understanding.
> Who determined its measurements — surely you know!
> On what were its bases sunk,
>   or who laid its cornerstone,
> when the morning stars sang together,
> and all the children of god shouted for joy?" (38:1–7)

God will not be questioned by someone who cannot explain how all living things are upheld and nurtured in freedom: "Is it by your wisdom that the hawk soars, and spreads his wings toward the south?" When Job finally catches his breath, after God's first, two-chapter-long onslaught, he is stunned and humbled: "I have spoken once . . . but I will proceed no further." Earlier his hope was that someone in the court of heaven would speak up for him — a mediator, or advocate, or redeemer.

"For I know that my Redeemer lives, and at last he will stand upon the earth, and after my skin has thus been destroyed, then from my flesh I shall see God" (19:25–26). In the end he simply admits that before what he had known of God was by reputation: "by the hearing of the ear." Now that he has experienced the power of God directly, he is ready to admit that his questions were arrogant, that no purpose of God can be thwarted. He repents himself in dust and ashes.

In the prose epilogue, the anger of God is directed toward the self-righteousness of Job's so-called comforters. They are spared only because of Job's prayer for them. And then Job is given new herds and a new family. "And the Lord blessed the latter days of Job more than his beginning." To most of us, this seems terribly unsatisfying. It's one of the tensions in the text between the poetic dialogues, the impatient Job, and a prose frame in which the ending seems almost tacked on, as though to make him fit the old story and the old theology again.

The person we identify with is the impatient Job, protesting, angry over unmerited suffering. And that, of course, is the living origin of the book. It comes as a response to the great crisis of the Babylonian exile. Up to that point the prevailing orthodoxy was that of Job's friends: suffering is the result of sin. It was implicit in what the prophets preached: unless the nation repents, abandons idolatry, adheres to the covenant, relies on God and practices justice, it will suffer punishment.

When the fall of Jerusalem came in 587 B.C.E., there were those among the Judean exiles who must have wondered, "But what did *I* do, what did my innocent children do, to deserve this?" The idea of the sins of the previous generations being visited on the children no longer seemed just. The prophet Jeremiah in this era had to address the notion of the sins of the fathers being visited upon the children and denied that this was what God was doing. The exiles must have identified with the story of a righteous man being tested by God—but not with his patience; with his talking back.

It may be that the prose frame of the Book of Job is just a futile attempt by an orthodox editor to fit the impatient Job back into a pious sense of tit-for-tat justice. But it's not persuasive. The voice out of the whirlwind, and the condemnation of the friends, perhaps; but what kind of God runs special tests of character that involve killing whole families — even if a whole new one is provided to those few who might "pass" such a test?

For many moderns, the issue is put succinctly in a famous syllogism from MacLeish's *J.B.*:

> If God is God He is not good,
> If God is good He is not God,
> take the even, take the odd.

This is not the place to argue an entire philosophical theology or theodicy. Allow me to argue, however, that this is not the final word on the subject. Simply put, the patient Job is ultimately *wrong*. God's purposes *can* be thwarted; we do it all the time. So MacLeish is wrong, too.

One response to Job is to say that it's a mistake to understand God in terms of absolute goodness, or goodness defined in human terms. But I would say, along with many modern theologians — feminists, process theologians, biblical scholars — that what is most useful in the tensions of the book is the suggestion it holds that it is a mistake to define God only in terms of absolute control over history, or absolute power. Discussion of God in terms of absolutes has more to do with Greek philosophy than with the Bible. The Bible as a whole seems interested not in God as absolute, but as relational; not as static, but as dynamic; not as impassive, but as affected by what we humans do well or ill or leave undone.

The philosopher Charles Hartshorne, in a fine little book called *Omnipotence and Other Theological Mistakes*, argued that it can still make sense to talk about reality in theological terms, but not in terms of absolute power, only in terms of relationship and (often thwarted) love.[5]

Why is redemption delayed? Why is there suffering? One biblical response is that creation has been placed within the limits of time. As the Voice says from out of the whirlwind, "Where were you when I laid the foundations of the earth?" All the parts of creation, at every level, have been granted both relationship to every other part and a certain indeterminacy, or freedom. Cosmos and chaos are inter-related and a certain randomness is built in. Tornados or whirlwinds are good examples. They do not come because "God sends them." Calling them "acts of God," as we so often do, should probably be considered a kind of theological slander. The rain falls and the sun shines on the just and the unjust alike. To deny that is to take the position of Job's so-called friends. It's to speak as fundamentalists do when they treat AIDS as sent by God to punish people. It's just a way of bad-mouthing God on the way to blaming as a habit in life.

But it must be said that Job is not the only sufferer to be found in the Bible. So it would be a mistake to focus on his as the only experience relevant to the problem of evil. The broader witness is that there are at least three different types of suffering and evil—and so many combinations—and each requires a different response. Sorting them out isn't easy.

Job marks a beginning in the Hebrew tradition—a reluctant one—in acknowledging that *some suffering comes for no good reason at all.* It just happens, impersonally. It comes out of the whirlwind, as part of the nature of things. And to that kind of suffering, the best, perhaps the only practical, spiritual response does come around to those most impersonal of human virtues, patience and endurance.

But we shouldn't deny for one minute that there is other suffering and evil that is very personal in its origins. "Thou art the man!" says the prophet Nathan pointing his finger at David the king. Not all evil requires patience. Some requires righteous indignation, prophetic warnings, correction.

But there are dangers with pushing this too far, as well. First, before getting righteous, one should always remember, "there is none without sin; no, not one." Some of what we suffer does require acknowledging that we are implicated in the evils being experienced. It requires that inward response called repentance. What's done may be done, but the possibility of change, of spiritual growth and new beginnings, of redemption, need never be closed.

Lastly, we should recognize that confronting evil will never be popular or without cost. Even serving the moral possibilities within us can bring its own kind of suffering. The prophets get stoned, rejected, or crucified. There is suffering that comes to those who seek to overcome evil with good. And the best response to that suffering, which comes in the course of truly serving one's moral calling, can only be the highest virtues: faith, hope, and authentic love.

"Why do bad things happen?" For a variety of reasons:

1) Because there *is* randomness;
2) Because there *are* the sins of others *and* those we ourselves are implicated in;
3) Because there *are* costs in overcoming evil with good.

One spiritual task is to sort out the strands. The knots are complex. But finding the proper responses to our frustrations, to human suffering and evil, is a major theme in the Bible. In short, it is full of Wisdom.

Redemptions: The Literary Prophets

At the height of the Cold War and nuclear arms race, Richard Wilbur wrote a poem called "Advice to a Prophet."[2] It begins:

> When you come, as soon you must,
>> to the street of our city,
> Mad-eyed from stating the obvious,
> Not proclaiming our fall but begging us
> In God's name to have self-pity,
> Spare us all word of the weapons,
>> their force and range . . .

He says the prophet must, in essence, also invoke the awesome beauty of creation itself, and ask,

> What should we be without
> The dolphin's arc, the dove's return,
> These things in which we have seen ourselves
>> and spoken?

The central paradigm of the Bible is sometimes said to be "sin and redemption." As developed in later Christian theology, with "sin" often understood more as a condition than a mistake, and redemption immediately associated with the need for a redeemer, Christ, it can become a barrier to our understanding of the Hebrew prophets. Because like Wilbur's prophet, the eighth century Hebrew prophets also had a sense of "original blessing." They did not think humanity hopeless. They found varied metaphors for the possibility always held open — of redemption, in one form or another, from the consequences of our foolish actions.

Today we are surrounded by many other basic paradigms analyzing what is wrong and what is needed. Some are religious, some secular. Some have to do with our relationship to one another, to our inner lives, to the creation, or to the political and economic order. But whether we think the problem is oppression, self-delusion, addiction, repression, alienation, or whatever, it may help us in approaching the Hebrew prophets to realize that their varied analyses encompassed versions of all of these.

Because the prophets all denounced what they saw as concrete social and spiritual evils, they did not have a singular approach to "redemption." Taking a God's-eye point of view, they delivered varied warnings. They also proclaimed that history is open-ended and not fated, and that the Creator of that openness, in steadfast love for us creatures, could yet redeem us from the consequences of our foolishness, corruption, and evils, restoring us to right relationship with God and one another.

Moses is considered the first and greatest prophet, but the role of the prophet in Israel, as we have seen, came to challenge and counterbalance its kings and priests. Hearing Yahweh's call, daring to speak for God, the prophet challenged both rulers and conventional religionists to understand the *real* problems and their solution more deeply. Most of the earliest prophets did not have their words collected and preserved for us. Deborah, Samuel, Nathan, Elijah, Elisha, et al., appear only briefly in the narrative history that stretches from Joshua through Kings, so that in the Tanakh those books are known as "The Former Prophets."

But now we come to "The Latter Prophets," or the Literary Prophets — Isaiah, Jeremiah, Ezekiel, and the Twelve. (This is the order in the Tanakh; the Christian Bible inserts Lamentations after Jeremiah and Daniel after Ezekiel.) These are largely collections of oracles assembled, like most biblical texts, after the Exile and long after their original composition. Tradition arranged them in order of their size. Isaiah has sixty-six chapters, Jeremiah fifty-two, Ezekiel forty-eight. The scroll of the Twelve consists of smaller prophetic books that range in length from fourteen chapters to a mere twenty-one verses. For their brevity, the Twelve have been called "minor" prophets, but they include major voices in the development of the prophetic tradition.

The nature of that development justifies a more chronological arrangement here. These oracles were preserved even when the very destruction they had feared came to pass. During and after the Exile, some were expanded, with more extensive hopes now appended. Eventually, prophetic proclamations of redemption were supplanted by expectations of messianic hope and then with apocalyptic vision, and the age of the Hebrew prophets came to an end.

AMOS: IN PROSPERITY, A MORE UNIVERSAL PERSPECTIVE

The earliest of these figures is Amos, a powerful voice arising from humble origins to challenge the complacency of the privileged. He was not born or educated for such a task. "I am no prophet, nor a prophet's son, but I am a herdsman, and a dresser of sycamore trees, and the Lord took me from following the flock, and the Lord said to me, 'Go, prophesy to my people Israel'" (Amos 7:14). So he went from his little village of Tekoa, in Judah, to the capital of the Northern Kingdom, then at Bethel. He makes this speech in a dramatic confrontation with the high priest there, Amaziah.

This was during the long reign there of King Jeroboam II (786–746 B.C.E.). As Amos depicts things, times were prosperous. Bethel had become wealthy, proud, and corrupt. The rich had palaces adorned with ivory. They had vineyards and anointed themselves with precious oils. At the same time, the poor were sorely afflicted, exploited, even sold into slavery, under corrupt judges. Although he begins by pronouncing God's judgments on the surrounding nations for their various transgressions against justice, to put things in more universal perspective, he soon zeroes in on Israel. He preaches at the city gate. He shares a vision of God standing on a wall, dropping a moral plumb line and warning that "the high places of Isaac shall be made desolate and the sanctuaries of Israel shall be laid waste."

Amos confronts the priests; he calls the well-to-do women of the city "fat cows of Bashan." He makes me want to get up on the hood of a Lexus in some posh suburban shopping mall, asking everyone (regardless of gender), to consider the consequences of conspicuous consumption — to the poor, to the planet. He warns that being chosen by Yahweh means being chosen to moral responsibility, not exemption from accountability (3:2).

In his day there had arisen a widespread belief in a coming "day of the Lord." To most Israelites it meant a time when Yahweh would make Israel dominant and triumphant again. But Amos warns, "Woe to you who desire the day of the Lord! . . . It is darkness, and not light!" Then he compares God to a devouring lion. In another vision, of a basket of summer fruit, he delivers God's warning, that what awaits Israel, in a time of abundance, is rot and ruin.

"Woe unto those who are at ease in Zion," thunders the prophet, "for you have turned judgment into gall, and the fruit of righteousness into wormwood" (Amos 6:1,12 KJV). The well-off are outwardly religious, but Amos despises their part-time piety: "Hear this, you who trample upon the needy, and bring the poor of the land to ruin, saying, 'When will the new moon be over, that we may sell grain? And the sabbath, that we may offer wheat for sale, that we may make the bushel small and the shekel great, and deal deceitfully with false balances, that we may buy the poor for silver and the needy for a pair of sandals, and sell the refuse of the wheat?'" (8:4–6 NRSV).

On God's behalf he says, "I hate, I despise your feasts, and I take no delight in your solemn assemblies. Even though you offer me your burnt offerings and cereal offerings, I will not accept them, and the peace offerings of your fatted beasts, I will not look upon them. Take away from me the noise of your songs; to the melody of your harps I will not listen. But let justice roll down like waters, and righteousness like an ever-flowing stream" (5:21–24).

It is likely that Amos was expelled from Israel and returned to Judah, where his oracles and preaching were set down and preserved. Among them was a warning that prophetic utterance would again be needed: "Behold, the days are coming," says the Lord God, "when I will send a famine on the land; not a famine of bread, nor a thirst for water, but of hearing the words of the Lord" (8:11). A later editor ended the collection similarly: "Behold, the days are coming, says the Lord, when . . . I will restore the fortunes of my people Israel, and they shall rebuild the ruined cities and inhabit them" (9:13f). The dominant tone is one of warning, but the hope is always for a return to the covenant. So the possibility of hope, of redemption from the consequences of evildoing, is never very far away.

HOSEA: GOD WILL REMAIN FAITHFUL,
EVEN TO THE UNFAITHFUL

This prophetic message of divine faithfulness and compassion, rather than divine wrath, is characteristic of Hosea, whose prophetic career came shortly after that of Amos and was also addressed to the Northern Kingdom of Israel. Hosea, however, spoke not as an outsider but as a native. Beginning shortly before the death of Jeroboam II in 746 B.C.E., he saw Israel descend quickly from stability into near anarchy. In the next two decades five kings reigned in Israel; four died by assassination. The Assyrians took Damascus in 733 and captured Samaria in 721, ending the Northern Kingdom.

To Amos, the chief sin is injustice. To Hosea, it is unfaithfulness to Yahweh — idolatry. Amos inveighs against evil deeds in contrast to outward piety. Hosea decries the absence of authentic spirituality: "For I desire steadfast love (hesed) and not sacrifice, attachment to God rather than burnt offerings" (6:6). In considering the past, Amos emphasizes what Yahweh had done; Hosea, what God has also felt: "When Israel was a child, I loved him, and out of Egypt I have called my son" (11:1). Now, however, "there is no loyalty, no love, no knowledge of God in the land; there is swearing, lying, killing, stealing and committing adultery" (4:1–2). They have set up a calf-idol in Samaria and perform pagan sacrifices on the hilltops. Having sown the wind, "they shall reap the whirlwind" (8:7).

Hosea portrays this in a very personal way. He considers God to be like a faithful husband whose wife has betrayed him. So when the word of Yahweh first comes to him, he is told to marry a woman with the disposition of a harlot. Then he gives her children prophetic names, as God instructs him: "Call her name Not-Pitied, for I will no more have pity on the house of Israel," and "Call his name Not-My-People, for you are not my people and I am not your God" (1:6, 8). And when she seems to have sold herself to someone else, Hosea redeems her for a price (3:2). He does not abandon her. The overall message is that neither will God abandon a steadfast love for Israel. Even though the nation may have to face the consequences of its faithless actions, the possibility of redemption always remains: "Come, and let us return unto the Lord; for he hath torn, and he will heal us; he hath smitten, and he will bind us up. After two days he will revive us; in the third day he will raise us up, and we shall live in his sight" (Hos. 6:1–2 KJV).

THE FIRST ISAIAH

Even more visionary is the first of the prophets whose oracles make up the scroll of Isaiah. Scholars have long noted that the lengthy collection comes from two different eras. Chapters 40 to 66 have references from after the Exile, in the time of Cyrus of Persia (539 B.C.E.). These latter Isaiahs are very important. The Isaiah behind chapters 1 to 39, however, is a great prophet as well, whose oracles were first delivered in the mid eighth century B.C.E., in Jerusalem, during the final year of the forty-year reign of King Uzziah of Judah (783–742 B.C.E.). The first Isaiah may have been a priest with prophetic vision, because in that year, apparently in the Temple, he reports having a vision of Yahweh (Isa. 6:1–8):

> I saw the Lord sitting upon a throne, high and lifted up; and his train filled the temple. Above it stood the seraphim; each one had six wings: with two he covered his face, and with two he covered his feet, and with two he flew. And one called to another and said:
>   "Holy, holy, holy is the Lord of hosts;
>   the whole earth is full of his glory."
> And the foundations of the thresholds shook at the voice of him who called, and the house was filled with smoke. And I said, "Woe is me! For I am lost, because I am a man of unclean lips and I dwell in the midst of a people of unclean lips; for my eyes have seen the King, the Lord of hosts." Then flew one of the seraphim to me, having in his hand a burning coal from the altar. And he touched my mouth, and said, "Behold, this has touched your lips; your guilt is taken away, and your sin forgiven." And I heard the voice of the Lord saying, "Whom shall I send, and who will go for us?" Then I said, "Here am I! Send me."

This vision is a classic expression not only of the prophet's call, but also of religious experience generally in the biblical tradition. It encompasses awe, a sense of sin and unworthiness, of purgation and acceptance, and, finally, of responsibility. According to the typology used by William James in his classic study *The Varieties of Religious Experience,* it is closer to a "twice-born" experience than to the "once-born" growth experiences preferred by self-reliant skeptics, religious liberals, and many modern seekers. More typical of that mode is Isaiah's earlier vision, of Yahweh's influence being universalized, creating peace:

> It shall come to pass in the latter days, that the
> mountain of the house of the Lord
> shall be established as the highest of the mountains,
> and shall be raised above the hills; and all the
> nations shall flow to it,
> and many peoples shall come, and say,
> "Come, let us go up to the mountain of the Lord, to
> the house of the God of Jacob; that he may teach us
> his ways, and that we may walk in his paths."
> For out of Zion shall go forth the law, and the word
> of the Lord from Jerusalem.
> He shall judge between the nations,
> and shall decide for many peoples;
> and they shall beat their swords into plowshares,
> and their spears into pruning hooks;
> nation shall not lift up sword against nation,
> neither shall they learn war any more (Isa. 2:2–4 KJV).

In this vision of the day of the Lord, the humble shall be lifted, the haughty brought low (2:12). But the prophet is not just casting a far-off vision. He is responding, as prophets always do, to a very concrete historical situation. He not only condemns injustice and faithlessness (1:4), and mere formality in religion, telling the people, "cease to do evil; learn to do good; seek justice, correct oppression, defend the fatherless, plead for the widow" (1:16–17). He condemns the rich "who join house to house, who add field to field" (5:8), but holds out the possibility of redemption as always close at hand:

> "Come now, let us reason together," says the Lord:
> "though your sins are like scarlet,
> they shall be white as snow;
> though they are red like crimson,

they shall become wool.
If you are willing and obedient,
   you shall eat the good of the land.
But if you refuse and rebel,
   you shall be devoured by the sword."
For the mouth of the Lord has spoken (2:18–20).

"Woe to those who call evil good and good evil, who put darkness for light, and light for darkness . . . woe to those who are wise in their own eyes, and shrewd in their own sight!" (5:20–21). In Isaiah's day, the Northern Kingdom had formed an alliance with Damascus. The prophet condemns all such foreign entanglements, both when King Ahaz of Judah turns to Assyria for help and when his successor, Hezekiah, relies on Egypt for a time. Yahweh is to be the nation's only external help, a calm and sure reliance on God alone, the only hope. "Take heed, be quiet, do not fear, and do not let your heart be faint, because of these two smoldering stumps of firebrands," he says. God will give a sign to the house of David when "a young woman shall conceive and bear a son, and shall call his name Immanuel," that is, "God is with us" (7:14). And later (9:2, 6),

The people who walked in darkness
   have seen a great light;
   Those who dwelt in a land of deep darkness,
   on them the light has shined . . .
For unto us a child is born, a son is given;
   and the government will be upon his shoulder,
   and his name will be called
   Wonderful Counselor, Mighty God,
   Everlasting Father, Prince of Peace.

This passage originally was an oracle at the coronation of a king of Judah, probably Hezekiah. But anyone who has ever sung or heard Handel's *Messiah* is familiar with these words and knows that later Christian tradition applied them to Jesus. These as well, which come from a period when the Davidic monarchy seemed reduced to a mere stump (11:1–2):

There shall come forth a shoot
    from the stump of Jesse,
and a branch shall grow out of his roots.
And the Spirit of the Lord shall rest upon him,
    the spirit of wisdom and understanding,
    the spirit of counsel and might,
    the spirit of knowledge
        and the fear of the Lord.

Holding forth hope, Isaiah prophesied of a day when "The wolf shall dwell with the lamb, and the leopard shall lie down with the kid, and the calf and lion and the fatling together, and a little child shall lead them . . . They shall not hurt or destroy in all my holy mountain; for the earth shall be full of the knowledge of the Lord, as the waters cover the sea" (11:6,9).

Many of Isaiah's oracles are directed against the injustices of the surrounding nations. Alliances with them will not help. "For thus said the Lord God, the Holy One of Israel, 'In returning and rest shall you be saved; in quietness and trust shall be your strength'" (30:15). He counsels King Hezekiah, but he predicts correctly where it will all end: "Behold, the days are coming, when all that is in your house, and that which your fathers have stored up till this day, shall be carried to Babylon; nothing shall be left, says the Lord" (39:5). Only a remnant shall be saved.

Yet this first Isaiah also begins to anchor his hope beyond all the agonies of human history. He envisions a Day of the Lord when God "will swallow up death for ever, and the Lord God will wipe away tears from all faces" (25:8). Such visions are called "eschatological" because they have to do with the End Time (Greek: *eschaton*). After this Isaiah, such visions become an increasingly important part of the prophet's role — which is not only to warn, but also to sustain: "to comfort the afflicted, as well as afflict the comfortable," as Reinhold Niebuhr put it during the Depression and World War II; to "strengthen the weak hands and make firm the feeble knees," as Isaiah phrases it (35:3). The effective prophet, then, is not merely a moralist, an ethicist, but also a person of faith, for whom the moral covenant can only be renewed through faith in the more basic covenant of being.

MICAH: WHAT YAHWEH REQUIRES OF YOU

Micah was a younger contemporary of Isaiah and prophesied both the destruction of Samaria and the eventual fall of Jerusalem. He came from Judah, but not the capital, and did not have Isaiah's high-placed connections. No single verse of the Bible better sums up the basic requirements of prophetic religion than his final comment on true worship:

"He has showed you, O man, what is good; and what does the Lord require of you but to do justice, and to love *hesed*, and to walk humbly with your God?" (Micah 6:8).

After the Exile some oracles were added to Micah's collection. These share the vision of a day when "nation shall not lift up sword against nation; neither shall they learn war any more; but they shall sit every man under his vine and fig tree, and none shall make them afraid." There is a tolerant, commonsense universalism in this Micah that sometimes seems missing in earlier prophets. "For all the peoples walk each in the name of its god, but we will walk in the name of the Lord our God, for ever and ever" (4:5).

JONAH: THE RELUCTANT AND PETULANT PROPHET

It speaks well for the editors who finally assembled the literary prophets that they knew the need for a little redemptive humor. The story of the prophet Jonah provides some. Although most scholars date this parable, or satire, as late, around 350 B.C.E., because it has to do with a prophetic ministry aimed against the Assyrian capital, Nineveh, the setting is in the eighth century. So it can be read as a commentary of the classical prophets. The story is meant to be funny, a point that is often lost on those who take it literally.

Jonah is told by Yahweh to go to Nineveh and denounce the city. Reluctant to go where he knows his message is not wanted, Jonah takes ship in the very opposite direction — toward Tarshish, a region we now know generally as the Riviera! Jonah reminds me of two young missionaries I once picked up hitchhiking. "Where are you going?" I asked.

Eventually they admitted that the Lord was sending them to start a new branch of their church—in Acapulco! (Here I am Lord—send me!)

When a storm threatens the ship, Jonah's guilty conscience prompts him to suggest that his shipmates throw him overboard to appease God. All most people know about Jonah is that he was "swallowed by a whale." Well, it ain't necessarily so! As William Jennings Bryan pointed out to Clarence Darrow at the Scopes trial, all the Bible really says is that it was "a great fish."[3] From the belly of which Jonah eloquently prays, in words that may have originally been an independent psalm of thanksgiving: "What I have vowed, I will pay. Deliverance belongs to the Lord!" (2:9). "And the Lord spoke to the fish, and it vomited Jonah out upon the dry land" (2:10). But when he keeps his vow, and goes to Nineveh and preaches repentance, a strange thing happens: the city actually *does* repent!

So Jonah's prophecy that the city will be destroyed for its sins does *not* come true. Angry at God for this, Jonah sits staring at the city. God makes a bush grow to give him shade. He's momentarily grateful. But when it dies he is angry again—enough to want to die himself. Hm! Says the Lord, "You get angry about a bush, for which you did not labor and which you did not grow; it came in a night and perished in a night. And I shouldn't be concerned about a big city like Nineveh, in which there are 120,000 people who don't know their right hand from their left, and lots of livestock?" (Jon. 4:10–11).

In synagogues, Jonah is read on the holiest day of the year, Yom Kippur. The point is that God's mercy to others is not something we should resent. Who knows, we might just need a little ourselves sometime!

JEREMIAH: JUSTICE ON EARTH, BUT COMPASSION TOWARD GOD

Compassion for ourselves is one thing, compassion toward our fellow humans, another; but compassion toward God? One reason we have trouble understanding the prophets is that this idea rarely occurs to us. Rabbi Abraham Joshua Heschel often said that after the Holocaust the notion of faith as comfort and sweetness simply had to be replaced by arduous compassion, including compassion for God, whose intentions toward humanity are so often perverted by humans. Judging by his great introduction to the biblical prophets, his precedent for this lies chiefly with Jeremiah.

The only way to understand Jeremiah, suggested Heschel, is to read him as expressing an almost unendurable identification with the rejected love, the sorrow and the anger of God when repeatedly rebuffed, ignored, and rejected. This leads to tremendous inner tension. On the one hand, vivid expressions of despair and lamentation over an unrepentant people, along with thundering denunciations of them continuing in evil, faithless ways; on the other hand, the persistence of God's love, and the ever-present possibility of authentic repentance and redemption. Puritan sermons often had this character, and were called *jeremiads*.

Jeremiah himself, however, was not always quite so high-pitched in his religious rhetoric. He was the son of the priest Hilkiah, who may be the same priest/prophet called upon by King Josiah in 622 B.C.E. to authenticate the scroll of the Law that had been "found" in the Temple. As a young man whose call to be a prophet came five years later, he may have taken a leading part in the Deuteronomic reform movement that followed. Richard Elliott Friedman believes that Jeremiah and his scribe, Baruch, were part of the circle that pulled together the D strand of the Bible, including the Deuteronomic history.

After the death of King Josiah, in 609 B.C.E., whatever influence Jeremiah had had in the capital was largely lost. In any case, he had found real reform and repentance rather rare. He began telling people that the threat of imminent destruction was a just punishment for the nation's ongoing, present sins. Not for the sins of its past. Jeremiah sets aside the old proverb that "the fathers have eaten sour grapes and the children's teeth are set on edge" (31:29).

He announces that the Babylonian armies will be the instruments of God's wrath. He denounces other prophets who say "peace, peace," where there is no peace. He is seen as a traitor. At various times he is put under house arrest, put in the stocks, thrown into an empty cistern, and banished.

His oracles of denunciation seem harsh and relentless. Yet every time he declaims, "Thus sayeth the Lord" behind it there is a pained plea,

"Please, please people: try to feel how God must feel when you continue this way!" He also never ceases to hold out the promise of a loyal, redeemed remnant, and of a new covenant—not merely signed by an outward circumcision, but by an inward circumcision of the heart: "Behold, the days come, says the Lord, that I will make a new covenant with the house of Israel . . . I will put my law in their inward parts, and write it in their hearts, and will be their God, and they shall be my people. And they shall teach no more . . . saying, know the Lord; for they shall all know me, from the least of them unto the greatest" (31:31,34).

When Jerusalem fell, Jeremiah was carried off not to Babylon, but with those who took refuge in an even more ironic place for God's people to go: Egypt. He seems to have died there. Before leaving Jerusalem, however, he and Baruch send a letter to the exiles in Babylon. It tells them that God knows that their hurt is uncurable and their wound grievous; that there is no one to uphold their cause and no healing (30:12–13). But it also promises that those who have devoured shall in turn be devoured, that the Exile will last only seventy years, and that then there will be a return and a restoration. How else could the prophetic tradition deal with what must have felt, and which it recorded, as the end, the finish, of its sacred history? How else but with hopes and vision anchored beyond history?

Expectations: Messianic Hopes and Apocalyptic Visions

꙳ ꙳ ꙳ ꙳

EZEKIEL: VISIONARY PRIEST AND PROPHET

A contrast to Jeremiah's experience can be found in his contemporary, Ezekiel. In the fifth year of the Babylonian captivity, on the banks of the river Chebar in Babylon, "the word of the Lord came expressly unto Ezekiel the priest." "The heavens were opened, and I saw visions of God" (1:1–3). The first of these is the vision of a wheel, connected to the throne chariot of God. The priest is then told to eat a scroll containing "lamentations, and mourning, and woe," but to him it tastes "as sweet as honey" because it is the word of God (2:3–3:3).

Ezekiel is customarily addressed by God as *ben 'Adam*, "son of man." Unlike Jeremiah, his message is not primarily a plea for repentance, but rather symbolic and parabolic visions that interpret the punishments that have already fallen on Israel. In one vision, he sees the *Kavod*, or very glory of God, being withdrawn from the Temple in Jerusalem. Not that he was better received than Jeremiah or felt more understood: "Ah, Lord God, they are saying of me, 'Is he not just another maker of allegories?'" (20:49). At last, however, God gives assuring news to deliver: to vindicate his own holy name, and not their sake, God will cleanse Israel of uncleanness, take out its heart of stone, give it a heart of flesh, and put his spirit in the people, cause them to observe his statutes, and return to the land (36:22–38).

This is followed by the famous vision of the valley of the dry bones in Ezekiel 37. God will put flesh on the dead again. Here we find the beginning of the belief in resurrection. In a tradition that had long avoided much concern for what happens after death, the Exile had provoked a visionary belief in the possibility of God giving new life. Finally, Ezekiel offers visions of Israel returning to Jerusalem and the Temple being rebuilt.

SECOND AND THIRD ISAIAH:
THE COMING OF THE MESSIANIC AGE

Perhaps the most beloved and comforting prophecies come from another prophet of exile, Second Isaiah, whose oracles begin with "Comfort ye, comfort ye, O my people" (40:1), as the text of Handel's *Messiah*
has it. This prophet, who either identified himself with or was associated with the spirit of the earlier Isaiah, does indeed begin to speak of a
meshiach, or anointed one of God, who will save Israel. In one sense,
this messiah is already a present reality — in the person of King Cyrus
of Persia, who is named as such: "Thus says the Lord to his anointed, to
Cyrus" (45:1).

It was Cyrus who conquered Babylon and permitted the Israelites to
return to Jerusalem. Isaiah himself does not seem much interested in
the idea of a messiah in the sense of a new descendent of David who will
be king of Israel, but popular expectations later came to focus there, as
the gospels make clear. Likewise, the Servant Songs of Second Isaiah,
along with the Psalms, played a critical role in the way the followers of
Jesus interpreted the meaning of his suffering and death. Indeed, this
part of Isaiah is sometimes referred to as "the fifth gospel."

When we read of the suffering Servant in Isaiah 53, that "he was
despised and rejected by men; a man of sorrows, and acquainted with
grief…" it is almost impossible to separate the familiar words from the
christological interpretation put on them by the gospels and by Handel's oratio. The exilic prophet, however, was clearly speaking about the
experience of Israel as a people. The Servant throughout the songs is
not some future individual, but "Jacob my servant, Israel whom I have
chosen" (44:1).

The gospels also portray Jesus as having his own self-understanding
shaped by the poetry in the scroll of Isaiah. In the gospel of Luke,
4:16–30, he is portrayed as delivering his first public address as a sermon on a text from Isaiah 66:1–3:

> The Spirit of the Lord is upon me,
> because the Lord has anointed me
> to preach good tidings to the meek;
> he hath sent me to bind up the brokenhearted,

> to proclaim liberty to the captives,
> and the opening of the prison to those who are bound.
> To proclaim the acceptable year of the Lord,
> and the Day of our God; to comfort all that mourn . . .
> to give unto them beauty for ashes,
> the oil of joy for mourning,
> the garment of praise for the spirit of heaviness,
> that they might be call trees of righteousness,
> the planting of the Lord . . .

Like this oracle, the final chapters of Isaiah may in fact come from a Third Isaiah, living during and after the Exile, who also declares God's intention to create a new heaven and a new earth (Isa. 65:17). "The wolf and the lamb shall feed together, and the lion shall eat straw like the bullock, and dust shall be the serpent's food. They shall not hurt or destroy in all my holy mountain" (65:25). During and after the Exile, perhaps influenced by a cosmic dualism learned from the Persians, perhaps just under the force of circumstances, historical prophecy increasingly gives way to expectations of a messianic age, to apocalyptic visions that are focused even beyond history itself.

THE END OF PROPHECY

The end of the classical age of prophecy can be seen in such post-Exilic prophets as Joel, Zechariah, Haggai, and Malachi. The role of the prophet loses its distinctiveness in the visions of these late prophets. As we have already seen, Joel prophesies that God will pour out his prophetic spirit on everyone, young and old, male and female, rich and humble. Everyone shall see visions.

Since prophets like Haggai and Zechariah share a great interest in rebuilding the Temple, their role also begins to blend in again with the religious and civic establishment. It is no longer public oracles of warning and reassurance that are the heart of their message, but rather exhortations based on visions that have been revealed to the seer. These visions are apocalyptic (the word means "uncovering" in Greek) in the sense that their symbolic meaning requires explication—in Zechariah, by an angelic messenger.

"My messenger" is, in fact, the meaning of the name of the prophet called Malachi, who may be the last of the literary prophets not only in placement within the Bible but in chronology as well. He speaks of God as universal father, of the covenant having been corrupted and needing renewal, and of Elijah coming in advance of the Day of the Lord. Such themes were all later elaborated in Christian theology. So Christians were glad to have his words at the very end of their version of the Hebrew scriptures, right before the Gospels. In the Tanakh, of course, these are *not* the last words. The Writings follow the Prophets and include a number of books composed during the post-Exilic period.

EZRA AND NEHEMIAH

These two books were originally considered one. Together, they tell the story of the end of the Exile and the Return to Judea. Cyrus of Persia conquered the Babylonians in 539 B.C.E. Soon his empire extended from the borders of India to those of Greece. Persian policy toward subject peoples allowed for local autonomy and religious diversity. So the following year Cyrus issued a decree permitting the first Jews to return to Jerusalem. Sheshbazaar, a Jew with a Persian name, was to serve as governor of Judah.

Work began on reconstructing the Temple. Conflicts emerged, however. The returnees represented the aristocratic and priestly caste that had been exiled by the Babylonians. The poorer Jews who had remained behind in Judah were reluctant to see them restored to their lands or privileges. Rebuilding stopped and did not resume until around 522 B.C.E. With Zerubbabel, a descendent of the Davidic royal house, as governor, and a high priest named Joshua, and with the encouragement of the prophets Haggai and Zechariah, the Second Temple was completed in 516 B.C.E. It lacked the lost Ark of the Covenant and the grandeur of Solomon's building, but a degree of Jewish autonomy had been reestablished, under Persian hegemony.

The exiles did not all return at once. Only in 458 B.C.E, for example, does Ezra enter the story, as religious leader of a third wave of returnees. He had an immense impact. Jewish tradition regards him as a lawgiver and second in importance only to Moses himself. The modern scholar Richard Elliott Friedman argues that it was Ezra, or his circle, who served as the definitive redactor of the Torah and gave the Pentateuch its textual configuration.

Distressed at how many Jews had intermarried, Ezra banned mixed marriages and banished foreign wives and their children. When reactions to his decree created difficulties, the Persian king, around 445 B.C.E., sent to Judah another Jewish official named Nehemiah to join him and to take particular responsibility for the rebuilding of the walls of Jerusalem. Nehemiah immediately became popular by ordering the cancellation of debts. When the rebuilding was completed, Ezra completed the rededication of Jerusalem by having the Torah read out to the people.

This Second Jewish Commonwealth soon took on aspects of a theocracy. While military and political power remained with the Persians and their appointees, the priests of the Second Temple exercised considerable influence and authority and represented Yahwism and Jewish spiritual autonomy. The countervailing voice of prophecy, so spiritually important under the Davidic kings, fell largely silent. What began to replace it, in a sense, was the Torah itself and its exposition in local assemblies. During the period of the Second Temple — especially during the Hellenistic period — the synagogue developed. As a result of the destruction of the Temple and the Exile, some Jews in the diaspora had established alternative local temples for the worship of Yahweh. More important, however, even in the land of Israel, were local assemblies of lay people, without the need for priests to perform sacrifices, where the sacred stories were recited or read, commented upon, and where the people could come to chant psalms and pray in common worship. One might add that synagogue worship eventually becomes the basis of church worship.

ESTHER AND DANIEL

Yet some Jews in exile had clearly retained little but an ethnic identification with their religion. The Book of Esther illustrates this. Set in the Persian capital, it does not even contain the word "God." As a result, later rabbis were reluctant to include it as scripture, but eventually did so because it served as the scroll the people wanted read aloud on a national holiday, held in the late winter or early spring. Less history than a legend, Esther purports to tell the origins of Purim, the holiday brought home to Palestine by returning Jews under Persian domination.

At the Persian royal court, Queen Vashti has been deposed for refusing to appear when summoned by the king. After a nationwide beauty contest the beautiful Esther (or Hadassah) is selected to replace her. A Jewish orphan raised by her cousin, Mordechai, she hides her identity as a Jew. This proves useful when Mordechai offends the king's chancellor, Haman, by refusing to bow down to him, and Haman orders reprisals against all the Jews. Esther intervenes. "Haman . . . had plotted against the Jews to destroy them, and had cast Pur, that is, the lot, to crush and destroy them; but when Esther came before the king, he gave orders in writing that his wicked plot he had devised against the Jews should come upon his own head, and that he and his sons should be hanged on the gallows. Therefore these days are called Purim, from the term "Pur" (Esther 9:24–26).

If Esther is the book of the Bible without God, Daniel is a book that pretends to know a bit too much about what God has in mind and sets a somewhat dangerous pattern, with its "apocalyptic" visions of the future. It presents itself as a narrative about a prophet at the court of Babylon and then under the Persians. In the Christian Bible it is placed after Ezekiel. But for the Tanakh, it is not part of the Nevi'im (Prophets) but part of the Ketuvim (Writings). That is both because Daniel illustrates the transition between prophetic and apocalyptic literature and because it really comes from a later period, the second century B.C.E., when Jews were suffering religious persecution under the Hellenistic king, Antiochus Epiphanes.

Daniel's emphasis is less on the prophet's work of reading the signs of the times so as to encourage a new course of human action within history and more on providing persecuted people who have despaired over history and feel abandoned by God with revelations concerning the end time and new divine initiatives that will set things right. Signs are found less in historical events than in visions, dreams, or the heavens, and in the deciphering of cryptic writings as though they were code-books — a process still very popular among biblical literalists when dealing with the symbolic references of Daniel and its later Christian counterpart, Revelation.

The stories in Daniel indeed reveal much about how concerned its writers were simply with issues of survival. Daniel survives in the lion's den. The faithful Jews, Shadrach, Meshach, and Abednego, miraculously survive in the fiery furnace. Daniel deciphers the handwriting on the wall at Belshazzar's feast, predicting that the king's end is near. Daniel's visions are largely eschatological; that is, they are concerned with the end of time and history itself, which seems increasingly near. They also express the expectation that God will send a messiah: "one like a son of man." With Daniel that phrase — which literally means simply a human being — becomes a virtual code word for an eschatological messiah: "I saw in the night visions, and behold, with the clouds of heaven there came one like a son of man, and he came to the Ancient of Days and was presented before him. And to him was given dominion and glory and [a] kingdom. . .that shall not be destroyed" (Dan. 7:13–14).

Since they purport to be products of the Persian period, when Jews had enjoyed relative religious and cultural autonomy, Esther and Daniel were written in Hebrew. Because they really date from the Hellenistic era, however, both also have additions in Greek, included in the Apocrypha.

JEWISH SCRIPTURES IN GREEK: THE APOCRYPHA

The Hellenistic era in the Near East began in 330 B.C.E., when Alexander the Great conquered Persia. After his death seven years later, Greek language and culture spread in influence throughout the region. Alexander's leading generals divided his empire. The Ptolemy dynasty established its capital at Alexandria in Egypt and the Seleucid dynasty at Antioch in Syria. The number of Jews living in just such diaspora cities, where Greek was the common language, by now probably exceeded the number left in Judea.

After a century under Egyptian Ptolemaic rule, Judea finally fell under the Syrian Seleucids in 201 B.C.E. By then many Jewish leaders, not only in the diaspora, but in the Jerusalem priesthood itself, were strongly influenced by Hellenistic culture. Jewish sacred writings had begun to appear in Greek. Some were included in the Alexandrian Greek translation of the Hebrew scriptures known as the Septuagint. As we saw in the chapter called "Versions," Catholic and Orthodox Christians came to include this material in the Bible itself, while Protestant reformers, like the rabbis, set aside those writings that did not have Hebrew originals.

The term *apocrypha,* first used by Jerome, means "things hidden away." The literary variety it encompasses is broad. The *First Book of Esdras,* for example, is a straightforward recapitulation of the history of the Exile, return, and rebuilding of Jerusalem and the Temple. It depicts Ezra reading and explaining the Torah (and praying against mixed marriage). The *Second Book of Esdras,* on the other hand, far from being historical, is an extravagant series of apocalyptic visions by a seer.

Tobit is a moralistic tale of a pious Jew who despite his good deeds has become blind and poor in Nineveh. God hears his prayer, however, and that of a demon-haunted woman named Sarah, and sends the archangel Raphael in disguise to help the blind man's son, Tobias, recover a deposit of his father's money, to marry Sarah, and heal his father's blindness. Before he dies, Tobit envisions the Temple rebuilt and Gentiles turning to the Lord God, burying all their idols.

Also set in the historical past, as an imaginative tale of resistance, is the story of Judith. When the Babylonian general Holofernes tries to starve a Jewish town into submission, the pious and beautiful widow uses her wiles to gain access to his tent, gets him drunk, and then dramatically decapitates the oppressor. To some degree this may be an expansion and update of the brief tale of Jael and Sisera told in the book of Judges. By this point in the development of the Bible most new additions build on something well established.

For example, the late collections of wisdom literature known as The Wisdom of Solomon and The Wisdom of Jesus ben Sirach (or Ecclesiasticus; not to be confused with Ecclesiastes) expand a genre that began with Proverbs. The traditions of Jeremiah are continued in a book attributed to his scribe, Baruch. It combines a confession of sin with a prayer for mercy, comfort, and consolation for Jerusalem, and an exhortation to seek Wisdom: "She is the book of the commandments of God and the law that endures forever." (Bar. 4:1) The so-called *Letter of Jeremiah* purports to be a copy of a message sent by the prophet to those who were to become exiles. It warns against worshiping powerless idols.

There are also liturgical and devotional poems like the *Prayer of Azariah* and the *Song of the Three Young Men*, plus the penitential *Prayer of Manesseh*. The Daniel traditions are extended through Susanna, an innocent heroine (her name means "lily" in Hebrew) who is falsely accused of adultery by two dirty old men, but is cleared in their separate interrogation by young Daniel. He is also the protagonist of the two fantastic tales known as *Bel and the Dragon*.

Finally, there are the several books of the Maccabees. The first starts with Alexander the Great. He and all his Hellenistic successors, like the Roman emperors after them, had a tendency to think of themselves in divine terms. When the Seleucid king, Antiochus IV Epiphanes ("God made manifest") fought the Ptolemies of Egypt in 169 B.C.E., he looted Jerusalem and its temple. He had already removed the reigning high priest and sold his office to his brother, who set about "reforming" Judaism by making it conform more to Hellenistic cultural norms. First Maccabees depicts Antiochus as commanding the Jews to cease such distinctive practices as Sabbath-keeping, circumcision, and the avoidance of animals and foods considered unclean, and finally, in 167 B.C.E., desecrating the Temple with a pagan altar, either to himself or to Zeus Olympios, "a desolating sacrilege" (1 Macc. 1:54) called by Daniel "the abomination of desolation."

A priest named Mattathias led a revolt against Antiochus, and his son Judas Maccabeus ("the Hammer") became leader of a guerrilla army that eventually prevailed against the Seleucid forces, recaptured Jerusalem, purified and rededicated the temple with an eight-day festival that became Hanukkah ("Dedication"). Perhaps because its later celebration includes the lighting of lamps, the legend developed that when the Maccabeans rekindled the eternal flame in the temple, they found only enough consecrated oil for it to burn for one day; miraculously, it burned for eight. You will not find this legend in First Maccabees, however, or even in the more miracle-friendly addition and retelling of this story that is Second Maccabees. Christian Orthodox Bibles also include a Third Maccabees, about persecution of Jews by the Ptolemy kings of Egypt, and a Fourth Maccabees, reflecting on the willingness of Jewish martyrs to die for their religion — but now from a Greek Stoic philosophical perspective.

JUDAISMS AND VARIED EXPECTATIONS

The term *ioudaismos* first appears in the Hellenistic era, designating those customs that distinguished the Jews from other peoples. Then as now, however, there were a wide variety of ways of being a Jew. Both sacred writings and secular history make that clear in the last centuries before the common era.

The successful Maccabean revolt had led to another period of relative Jewish autonomy. The family that had led the rebellion, the Hasmoneans, took up the office of high priest and king, starting with the brother of Judas Maccabeus, Jonathan, in 152 B.C.E. The dynasty endured roughly a century. Already in the fight against the Seleucids, however, the Hasmoneans had turned to the growing power of Rome as an ally (1 Macc. 15). In 63 B.C.E. the Roman general Pompey entered Jerusalem to resolve a Hasmonean dynastic dispute, making the winner a Roman client. Political and military control of the Near East passed to Rome, though the culture remained thoroughly Hellenistic, Rome itself having also been strongly influenced by Greek language and culture.

In 37 B.C.E., as a reward for his help in combating the Parthian Empire to the East, the Romans established a local strongman named Herod as king of the Jews, despite the fact that he came from non-Jewish, Idumean ancestry. In order to consolidate his power, Herod was not only ruthless with potential rivals, but co-opted the Temple priesthood by enormously expanding and beautifying the Jerusalem Temple, as well as building fortresses, aqueducts, and other public works throughout the land. He ruled as a client king over Roman Palestine for over forty years, dying in 4 C.E. After his son Archelaus failed at maintaining order, Rome exercised direct control over Jerusalem and Judea through a series of procurators dependent upon its governor of Syria, while allowing other descendents of Herod to rule east of the Jordan and over Galilee in the north.

Small-scale rebellions against Roman and Herodian rule, often religiously inspired, were frequent. Finally, in 66 C.E. a major Jewish rebellion broke out, which brought an entire Roman army to lay siege to Jerusalem. In 70 C.E. the Herodian Temple was destroyed. The last Jewish resistance forces took their own lives at the fortress of Masada in 73 C.E. The shock to Jews throughout the world was enormous. For the most part Roman law exempted Jews from having to pay homage to the imperial gods or violate their customs, but when diaspora Jews rebelled against Rome in 115–117 C.E., the Jewish community at Alexandria was decimated under Trajan. Then in Palestine in 132–135 C.E., a charismatic guerilla who called himself Bar Kokhba ("son of the star") was hailed as the messiah and managed to establish independence briefly, before his rebellion, too, was finally crushed.

Religiously, as one might imagine, Jews during this turbulent period took any number of stands in relation to Torah, tradition, and expectation. The Jewish writers Philo of Alexandria (ca. 15 B.C.E.to 50 C.E.) and Josephus (37 C.E. to 100 C.E.), as well as the Roman writer Pliny, all testify to the growth of various sects within first-century Judaism. Philo, who himself was strongly inclined to try to interpret the particulars of Jewish tradition in the universalizing and dualistic terms of Greek philosophy, reports on quasi-monastic communities of Jewish men and women called "Therapeutae," living near Alexandria in celibate, contemplative anticipation of heaven.

In Palestine, according to Josephus, the most important Jewish "schools of thought" were the Pharisees, the Sadducees, and the Essenes. The word "Pharisee" has acquired negative overtones through the antagonism displayed in the Christian gospels. Ironically, Jesus may have been closer to this group than to any other, as we shall see. They expected the resurrection of the dead. They believed in observing the Torah not just outwardly, but in one's inner intentions. Their name, probably given them by others, comes from a root meaning "separate, interpret," and they did both. They adhered both to the written Torah, which they continued to interpret, and to the oral traditions derived from it, and therefore set themselves somewhat apart from the nonobservant and the nonchalance toward religion prevalent in Hellenistic culture.

The term *Sadducee* may have been ironic, since it seems related to Zadok, the original Davidic high priest, but was applied to those who surrounded the non-Zadokite Temple priesthood from the Hasmoneans onward. Philosophically influenced by Hellenism, the Sadducees did not believe in the resurrection of the dead. They emphasized human free will over God's control of history.

The descriptions of the Essenes in Josephus and the other ancient writers are not entirely consistent with one another or with the contents of the scrolls found in 1947 at Qumran, near the Dead Sea. Yet it is now clear that the community that assembled that library should be identified with them. The term "Essene" may be related to a word for both priestly breastplate and oracles. Certainly the Qumran community was concerned with observing priestly purity and with eschatological expectations.

Its members, convinced that the Temple had become irredeemably corrupt, seem to have gone to the wilderness southeast of Jerusalem to "prepare the way of the Lord." The Qumran library, though not complete as it was hidden at the time of the Roman invasion of 68–70 C.E., includes at least portions of every book of the Hebrew scriptures, plus a number of writings more particular to the community. The "War Scroll" is an apocalyptic vision of coming cosmic conflict, cast in the strong contrast between images of light and darkness that characterize most Qumran piety. The Rule of the Community indicates that they marked the beginning of the end time by the withdrawal to the desert of twelve representative men who keep the law, plus three priestly figures, there to learn from a "Teacher of Righteousness" who is also the authentic high priest.

So Jewish messianic expectation by this time had multiple forms. The First Book of Enoch, an extra-canonical text originally composed in Aramaic — which had become the daily language of ordinary Jews in Palestine by this time — speaks of expecting a "son of man" as an eschatological messiah. Until it was destroyed, other expectations focused on the Temple and its priesthood. Still others harbored the hope that a descendent of David would reestablish the authentic monarchy and political autonomy. The most extreme of nationalists, known as Zealots, were willing to bring this about through violence. They blended in with brigands known as *sicarii,* or daggermen. We can only understand what develops next in the biblical tradition within this mix of conflicting expectations.

CHRISTIAN SCRIPTURES (NEW TESTAMENT)

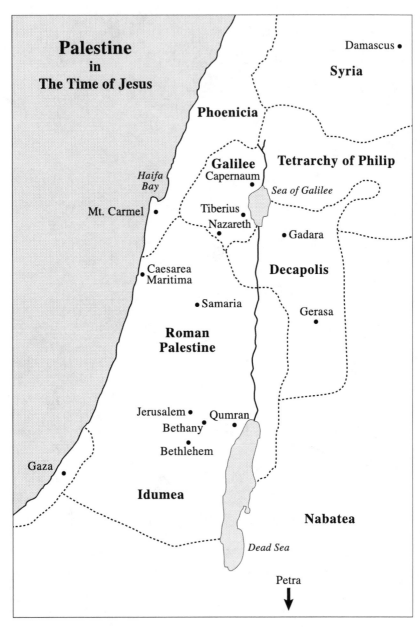

Judea, Samaria, and Galilee in the time of Jesus

A CHRONOLOGY FOR THE
CHRISTIAN SCRIPTURE

200 B.C.E.	Septuagint translation of Hebrew Bible into Greek
63 B.C.E.	Beginning of Roman era in Palestine
37 B.C.E.	Herod appointed King of the Jews by the Romans
4 B.C.E.	Birth of Jesus?; death of King Herod
4 B.C.E.–39 CE	Herod Antipas, ruler (tetrarch) of Galilee
6 C.E.	First Roman procurators replaced Herodian rulers of Judea
26–36	Pontius Pilate as Roman procurator of Judea
30	Crucifixion of Jesus
33–36	Paul joins the Jesus movement
50–63	Paul's seven authentic letters written
66–73	Galilee and Judea revolt against Rome
70	Roman destruction of the Temple in Jerusalem
70s	Gospel according to Mark
80s	Matthew and Luke–Acts
90s	Gospel according to John
70–100	DeuteroPauline, Pastoral, and Johannine Epistles
95–100	Revelation (Apocalypse of John)

ca. 100	Rabbinic canon of the Hebrew Bible
132–35	Bar Kokhba leads another Jewish revolt against Rome; persecutions
140–150	Marcionite controversy; catholic canon of New Testament
220–225	Rabbinic publication of the Mishnah
325	Council of Nicea under Emperor Constantine; Suppression of Gnostic and Arian heresies

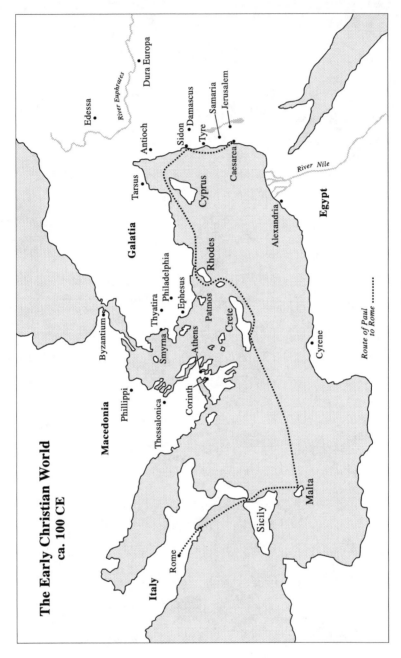

The Early Christian World
ca. 100 CE

The Eastern Mediterranean in the Early Christian period

Proclamations: Messages of the Kingdom and the Gospel According to Mark

The Hebrew Bible took form over a period of centuries. The Christian scriptures, only one-fourth as long, developed in a matter of decades, mostly between 60 and 110 C.E. They are written not in the classical Greek of Athens in the fifth century B.C.E., but in the common, Koine Greek that had become the shared written and commercial language of the Eastern Mediterranean. So the twenty-seven books that were eventually accepted as authoritative by Christians have only occasional vestiges of the Aramaic that Jesus and his original followers spoke in Palestine before his death around the year 30 C.E.

The Greek word *kerygma* means proclamation, preaching, or message. Within this literature we find a series of unfolding, but changing, proclamations:

‡ the message of John the Baptist: "Repent, for the kingdom of heaven is at hand." (Matt. 3:2)

‡ the message of Jesus concerning God's kingdom

‡ the proclamation of Jesus as the messiah, which led to his crucifixion by the Romans as "King of the Jews"

‡ after Jesus' death, the proclamation by his disciples of his resurrection

‡ the *kerygma* of Paul and other apostles as they spread "the Way" of Jesus among both Jews and Gentiles

‡ the formulation of the written gospels (between 70 and 90 C.E.) as manuals of teaching to assist those spreading the message

‡ pastoral proclamations about church discipline made in the name of Paul by a subsequent generation of leaders

‡ and finally, messages of encouragement, doctrinal definition, and hope by second-century Christians in the face of persecutions, heresies, and eschatological delay

Søren Kierkegaard once remarked that "life can only be understood backward; but it must be lived forward." The same could be said of reading these scriptures. The earlier messages in our series of proclamations come down to us in forms influenced by the concerns and rhetoric of the later generations. So we must read them with that in mind.

The New Testament is arranged with the gospels first. Then come the letters of Paul, other letters attributed to Paul, to his followers, and to apostles like Peter and John, ending with Revelation, or the Apocalypse of John. It has long been understood, however, that the gospels as proclamations are neither eyewitness accounts of Jesus nor even the oldest of the Christian scriptures. They were all composed between 70 C.E. and the end of the century, after the destruction of the Jerusalem Temple, and forty to seventy years after Jesus had died. The letters of Paul, composed between 50 C.E. and his death in the late sixties are actually older. It is also clear that the proclamation of a message *about* Jesus by Paul and others is what the gospels are about. The message *of* Jesus, whom Paul never even knew in the flesh, was surely transformed in the process.

For example, in "the parting of the ways" between the early church and the Jewish matrix from which it emerged, a good deal of anti-Judaism entered Christianity, inscribed in the scriptures themselves. Yet Jesus the Jew was hardly anti-Jewish, even when debating with the Pharisees, whose point of view on many matters was rather close to his own. Some elements of the early church, in order to make the Christian message more broadly acceptable within the Gentile world of the Roman Empire, also tended to generalize and "spiritualize" the message of Jesus, blunting not only its Jewish prophetic context, but the more specific social-political meaning of a kingless "Kingdom of God." The transmittal of the message necessarily involved interpretation. But all too often the privileges of shaping and articulating the message anew went to men with scribal power and leadership authority in a patriarchal society. So the voice, agency, and stories of women—an important part of the Jesus movement from its start—were minimized and marginalized. All of this more than justifies what feminist scholars call *a hermeneutic* [an interpretive strategy] of *suspicion* before we can begin to reconstruct the world and message of Jesus and of the earliest communities gathered in his name.

Scholars long ago saw that the gospel accounts require comparative study. They noted that three of the gospels—Matthew, Mark, and Luke—bear a structural similarity. Each has two main parts: a Galilee narrative focused on Jesus proclaiming God's Kingdom, then one set in Jerusalem at Passover, culminating in his death by crucifixion and in reports of his resurrection. Matthew and Luke each add differing birth narratives at the beginning, and at the end add more post-resurrection stories than Mark has, but otherwise they are parallel. They can be printed and read with the related texts side by side, so that they are called the *synoptic* gospels.

The Gospel of John stands apart in both structure and style. Jesus goes to Jerusalem several times, not just for his last Passover, as in the synoptics. He defines himself theologically in a series of "I am" sermons, while in the synoptics he hides his mission and identity and instead asks, "Who do *you* say that I am?"

German biblical scholars also noticed long ago that Matthew and Luke both repeat almost everything in Mark. Both also include some teachings of Jesus that are not in Mark. They hypothesized that Matthew and Luke had two documentary sources to work with: Mark, plus a common "sayings source," which they called "Q" (from the German *quelle*, or "source"). Q must have resembled the later Gospel of Thomas, a Gnostic document in which there is no passion narrative, only a series of teachings by Jesus. Many of the Q sayings have to do with the Kingdom of God.

More recently, scholarship has emphasized study not only of the texts, but of their contexts as well. Archeological and historical research have helped us to understand the peasant society of first-century Galilee and the urban life of Jerusalem and other Eastern Mediterranean cities where early Christian communities developed.[1] There have also been two major discoveries of libraries of religious texts not included in the Christian scriptures but illuminating some of the issues that bracketed the early Christian world.

The first was the 1947 discovery, near the Dead Sea, at a place called Qumran, of a library belonging to a Jewish sect that probably hid their texts at the time of the Roman siege of Jerusalem (68–70 C.E.). The religious context of first-century Judea has been illumined by publication of these so-called Dead Sea scrolls.[2] Their sectarian literature shows that the community at Qumran was intensely critical of the Temple establishment, both awaiting God's intervention and trying to anticipate the messianic age through a life of sharing, baptismal purification, communal meals, and righteousness. The second library dates from two centuries later. Found at Nag Hammadi in upper Egypt in 1945, these texts come from a third-century sect of Christian Gnostics — of whom more later.

Moreover, since World War II and the Holocaust, Christian scholars have been more motivated to examine the scriptural sources of anti-Semitism and to read both Jesus and Paul more as Jewish religious leaders. Studies of the early rabbinic tradition have helped even conservative Christian evangelicals to read Paul as doing an alternative form of *midrash*, in which the Messiah has already come, and to hear Jesus more clearly as doing *Jewish* theology.[3]

Indeed, one of the few things we know for certain about Jesus is that the Romans crucified him as "King of the Jews." Historian Paula Fredricksen points out that this form of death was distinctly Roman, not Jewish, and that it was used against those considered a threat to public order.[4] So though he was killed during the Passover festival at Jerusalem, probably in the year 30 C.E., it was not for strictly "religious" reasons, but as a political act of social intimidation. Note that Pontius Pilate did not find it necessary to round up the Galilean disciples of Jesus. In fact, many helped establish a community in Jerusalem itself. Since later Christology strained to explain why it had been necessary, it also seems likely that Jesus began his ministry after being baptized by John.

So let's begin there. What was it about John the Baptist's message that attracted Jesus and so many others? What did he mean in proclaiming the "Kingdom of God"? And how did Jesus continue or change John's message?

It is possible that John came from a poor, rural, priestly family that would have had reason to resent the opulence of the Jerusalem Temple. Luke includes such a suggestion as part of a highly stylized legend about

John's birth, which makes him a cousin to Jesus. Scholars reject the legend as history, but also note that John's eschatology and practice bears some similarities to that alternative priestly community at Qumran.

But it is the oldest and shortest of the gospels, Mark, that provides more of what we can reliably know about John: "John the Baptizer appeared in the wilderness preaching a baptism of repentance for the forgiveness of sins" (Mark 1:4). Matthew turns this into a direct message: "Repent, for the kingdom of heaven is at hand" (Matt. 2:2). Never mind for a moment how John is taken to be a forerunner for Jesus. The gospels, after all, are about the latter, not about the Baptist. Mark says "there went out to him all the country of Judea, and all the people of Jerusalem." Even if that's an exaggeration, John must have attracted enough followers so that he was considered a threat. Herod Antipas, the ruler of Galilee, had him arrested, probably in 26 or 27 C.E., and killed a year or two later. "For John said to Herod, 'It is not lawful for you to marry your brother's wife'" (Mark 6:18).

The story of that wife's daughter dancing for Herod and demanding the head of the Baptist on a platter is dramatic, but she is not named Salome in the gospels. The Jewish historian Josephus has to supply that fact, minus the dance. What he says about John is that he was "a good man" who "exhorted the Jews to lead righteous lives, to practice justice toward their fellows and piety toward God, and so doing join in baptism."[5]

Josephus understands that John's message was not merely about the ruler's marital morality, but about social justice. As a Romanized Jew, however, he tends to minimize the eschatological elements of John's prophetic preaching of "the kingdom." What it implies, after all, is that Caesar is not the ruler of the world; nor are the Herodians truly kings of the Jews. Only *God* is the ruler of the world. The faithful know that. God will soon prove it.

Proclamation of God's kingdom was not just theology then. It had social import. It had mass appeal especially among the poor. The peasant population was being oppressed by heavy taxation to pay Roman tribute and support the Herodians' ambitious building projects. The Temple in Jerusalem, exacting both tithes and a half-shekel tax on every Jew, supported a large, corrupt bureaucracy in opulence. Pious Jews known as Pharisees had separated themselves (that is what the word means) from all this and called for scrupulous adherence to the Law, both written and oral. Ordinary "people of the land" could not easily keep themselves as ritually pure as all the traditions required. Yet they knew their Bible. They passed on its stories orally and heard it read publicly and discussed in the synagogues.

The stories that Mark assembles may have circulated separately, and among such peasants, but they show a rich appreciation of biblical resonance. Take the baptism of Jesus by John, in the Jordan — with its biblical memory of waters passed through on the way from bondage to freedom, and to the fulfillment of God's promises. The opening of the heavens is an apocalyptic image. They had been closed with the end of prophecy, with God's voice no longer being heard. Now God's spirit descends as a dove, like the dove over the waters of the flood in Genesis. Jesus is declared "beloved Son" by a voice that speaks to him (not to the crowd, as when Matthew increases the drama). What blessing brings, however, is temptation: "The Spirit immediately drove him out into the wilderness. And he was in the wilderness forty days, tempted by Satan; and he was with the wild beasts; and the angels ministered to him." This passage evokes the forty years that Israel spent in the wilderness, the Satan who tests Job, Daniel protected from the lion, and angelic messengers and helpers to the prophets. Only after this, says Mark, "Jesus came into Galilee, preaching the gospel of God, and saying, 'The time is fulfilled, and the kingdom of God is at hand; repent, and believe in the gospel'" (Mark 1:14).

So John the Baptist's message of repentance is reframed as "good news." There are other discontinuities. Only in the Gospel of John do we get any report of Jesus baptizing anyone himself (John 3:22, 26). The synoptics portray him emphasizing not only what God *will* do, but what God is *already* doing. Some interpreters have called this a "realized eschatology": what God will eventually do, establish his kingdom fully, vindicating the righteous, is already happening. What will be already *is*— for those who have eyes to see, ears to hear, and hearts to understand.

In Mark's gospel, Jesus is portrayed as developing the proclamation of God's *dynamis* or power begun verbally by John not just by talking about it but in urgent action. Everything seems to be done "immediately." "Follow me," he says to the fishermen, Simon and Andrew, "and I will make you fishers of men. And immediately they left their nets and followed him" (1:18). "And they went into Capernaum; and immediately on the Sabbath he entered the synagogue and taught. And they were astonished at his teaching, for he taught them as one who had authority, and not as the scribes" (1:21–22). When Jesus teaches about the kingdom, it is often in parables drawn from everyday peasant life. Why does God's kingdom not spring up everywhere, right now? God is compared to a sower. Some seed falls on rocky ground, where it grows up quickly, but fails to take deep root and withers. Some is devoured by birds or choked by thorns. But some seed falls on good soil and yields a good crop. Yet only some understand, even after Jesus explains his meaning (Mark 4:3–20).

The demonstrations of God's power and authority are now in the form of exorcisms and healings. "And immediately there was in their synagogue a man with an unclean spirit; and he cried out, 'What have you to do with me, Jesus of Nazareth? Have you come to destroy us? I know who you are, the Holy One of God.' But Jesus rebuked him, saying, 'Be silent, and come out of him!' And the unclean spirit, convulsing him and crying with a loud voice, came out of him. And they were all amazed, so that they questioned among themselves, saying, 'What is this? A new teaching! He commands even the unclean spirits, and they obey him!' And at once his fame spread everywhere throughout all the surrounding region of Galilee" (Mark 1:23–28).

When some rebuke him for healing on the Sabbath, Jesus makes a very sound rabbinic argument that on the Sabbath it is lawful to do good and save life (Mark 3:1–6). When a crowd of five thousand stays late listening to him, the disciples want to send the people away to get food. But Jesus says, "You give them something to eat." They have only five loaves and two fish. But it proves enough and more (Mark 6:35–44). It is tempting either to explain such stories (everyone had some food tucked away and shared), or to read them as symbolic. Some probably are symbolic, like those of Jesus calming the storm and walking across the water ahead of the disciples' boat when they encounter a headwind (Mark 4:35–41; 6:45–52).

Israel has been possessed, paralyzed, blinded, deafened, crippled, fearful, and hungry; now it is to be sane, whole, sighted, empowered, faithful, and fed, by God! Such a reading sets the miracles within the later proclamation of the power and authority of Jesus by the evangelists. But even secular historians accept the idea that at least some of the stories, though told as "signs" of his authority as a healer in the prophetic traditions, probably began in memories of Jesus *acting* as such a healer and prophetic exorcist. He heals the paralytic by telling him, "Your sins are forgiven," which some consider blasphemy, since God alone can forgive sins (Mark 2:5–7). But he has no power to heal in his own hometown, since a prophet is not without honor except among his own people (Mark 6:4).

First told to help people believe, the miracle stories in their familiarity now threaten to become barriers to our hearing their deeper message. For even if Emerson was right when he said, "There is only one miracle"—life itself—these stories rebuke every form of human power over others as idolatrous and oppressive. They are about the Transcendent as the ultimate source of wholeness and justice in life.

Notice that when the unclean spirit identifies him as "the Holy One of God," Jesus commands it to keep silent (1:25). Mark also believes that Jesus is "the Son of God" (1:1). He has God say it at the baptism and when Jesus appears to his closest disciples transfigured along with Moses and Elijah (9:7). He has a Roman centurion confess it when Jesus is on the cross (15:39). Jesus refers to himself only with the ambiguous term "son of man." The "messianic secret" of Jesus' real identity becomes the key dramatic device in Mark's narrative, with the disciples only gradually discerning who he really is. The turning point comes when he asks, "Who do *you* say that I am?" and Peter answers, "You are the Christ," the anointed one (8:29).

Many historical scholars doubt that Jesus thought of himself in messianic terms, at least in Galilee.[6] They see the Jesus movement as a renewal movement within Israel, both expecting and living an eschatological faith in God as the only ruler.[7] The twelve disciples, one for each of the tribes of Israel, are to show that ordinary people will lead the way to this renewed sense of God's kingless kingdom.

But is that kingdom *only* for the children of Israel? No, says the dramatic story of the Syro-Phoenician woman (Mark 7:24–31). She importunes Jesus to heal her daughter. His first response to her is nothing short of insulting: "Let the children first be fed, for it is not right to take the children's bread and throw it to the dogs." She shames him into changing his mind, however. The whole story hardly makes Jesus look good. So there may be an authentic memory of his ministry behind it. On the other hand, it may, like the centurion, also reflect Mark's role in the spread of the Jesus movement to Gentiles.

In many respects Mark is the most liberating gospel for oppressed and marginalized groups.[8] It suggests that the kingdom involves a discipleship of equals. Those who want to be the greatest are told, "If any one would be first, he must be last of all and servant of all" (9:35). It threatens the very norms of patriarchal family life: "Whoever does the will of God is my brother, and sister, and mother" (3:33).

To be sure, it is an *androcentric* text, typical of its era, assuming men to be the norm, putting women at the margins of the story. Only toward the very end does Mark finally admit that there were many women "who, when he was in Galilee, followed him . . . and also many other women who came up with him to Jerusalem" (15:41).

Entering Jerusalem, he is hailed in the name of "the kingdom of our father David that is coming" (11:10). This interpretation of Jesus as a messiah who would reestablish the Jewish kingdom leads to his arrest. In order to consider what happens next, however, we must also reflect on the other gospels, especially the most familiar passion narratives, those told by Matthew and Luke.

Passions: The Teachings and Death of Jesus in Matthew and Luke

Recently I heard the stunning choral/orchestral *Pasion Segun Marcos*, by the multicultural composer Osvaldo Golijov. Born in Argentina to a Romanian Jewish mother and a Russian atheist father, Golijov wanted to create a work that would be as moving to a poor Catholic in Latin America as to a sophisticated despiser of religion in an urban concert hall. At the end, Jesus on the cross is sung to in Spanish by Mary Magdalene; he sings to the empty sky in Latin; while the chorus sings the Kaddish, the Jewish prayer of praise to the Creator said even in the face of death, in Aramaic. I was moved to tears.

The passion of Jesus has long inspired passionate works of art, by both believers and nonbelievers. The story reaches us on the shared human ground of suffering, which is what the Latin root of "passion" means, after all. I think of the *Pieta* by Michelangelo and the *Crucifixion* by Grünewald; *The Last Temptation of Christ*, by Kazantzakis, where passion has its other meaning as well; Pasolini's film *The Gospel according to Matthew*; and the great choral Passions by J. S. Bach.

Yet "passion" is also related to the word "passive." And the idea that passive suffering is redemptive I find profoundly problematic. Feminist theologians have begun actively to question whether it is helpful to continue to say that it is the suffering and death of Jesus that "saves."[1] All too often, they point out, women and the oppressed have been told to endure abuse in order to emulate Jesus—as though that is what the Human One wanted when he challenged every oppression in the name of God's coming commonwealth.

What did Jesus teach concerning suffering? Was it what he taught that led to his death? Or was it something else? The gospels by Matthew and Luke both expand Mark's story of the passion. They also include in the teachings of Jesus material from the lost "Sayings Source," Q. Understanding both better may help us with some tentative answers.

In Mark's telling, the passion is terse and poignant. Never understood even by his closest disciples, Jesus is increasingly isolated toward
the end. Most of the disciples run back to Galilee when he is arrested.
Even Peter denies ever having known him. At the end, if there is "salvation," it all still remains to be done. It somehow depends upon us. At
the end of Matthew and Luke, on the other hand, despite the suffering,
the victory has been won. It has been done. History has been changed.

It seems likely that Mark wrote in the midst of crisis—during or
just after the destruction of the Temple in 70 C.E. In Mark 13, Jesus is
portrayed as predicting that the Temple soon will be destroyed.
Matthew and Luke probably date from a decade or more later. Matthew
is more likely to be by a scribe in Antioch, who had collected the traditions of the Syro-Palestinian followers of Jesus, than by the disciple
who was elected to replace Judas in Acts 1:26. And Luke is more likely
to have been written in one of the largely Gentile Christian communities founded by Paul in Asia Minor, such as Ephesus, than by Paul's
sometime companion, "Luke the physician." Both write artfully, and
theologically, for particular audiences, but despite that one is sometimes less *with* Jesus in Galilee or Jerusalem around 30 C.E. than at a
liturgy *about* Jesus in Antioch or Ephesus in the eighties.[2]

Matthew's message is aimed at Jewish believers in Jesus as the Messiah. He is at pains to prove that Jesus descended from David, delivered
his teachings as a new Moses, fulfilled all the prophecies understood as
relevant, and died according to the scriptures, as the "suffering servant"
foretold by Isaiah. Luke's gospel is the first of a two-part work, continued in the Acts of the Apostles. He addresses a largely Gentile audience,
telling them that God sent his own son not merely to save Israel, but as
the savior and Lord of all people. It is in Luke that we most often hear
Jesus addressed as "Lord" (*kyrios*), while it is in Matthew that we most
often hear Jesus use for God the Aramaic term *Abba*, Father or Papa,
some twenty-one times. Both became part of the church's Christology, yet these gospels also incorporate traditions from the "Sayings
Source," Q, that suggest alternative understandings of Jesus—more as
Miriam's exodus child and as Wisdom/Sophia's prophet.[3]

For Luke, the mission of Jesus is declared in the first sermon he gives
in the Nazareth synagogue, on a text from Isaiah (61:1–3): "The spirit

of the Lord is upon me, for he has anointed me to preach good news to the poor. He has sent me to proclaim release to the captives and recovering of sight to the blind, to set at liberty those who are oppressed, and to proclaim the acceptable year of the Lord" (Luke 4:18–19). Matthew has Jesus define his mission in the first and greatest of the five discourses he artfully constructs. In the Sermon on the Mount (Matt. 5–7), this new Moses declares, "I have come not to abolish the Law, but to fulfill it" (Matt. 5:17). Luke offers a partial parallel text in his much shorter Sermon on the Plain (Luke 6:20–49). Both begin with a series of sayings that all begin with the phrase, "Blessed are . . ." These are known traditionally as "The Beatitudes."

Luke's version is political: "Blessed are you poor, for yours is the kingdom of God" (Luke 6:20). Matthew spiritualizes poverty and avoids using the name of G*d: "Blessed are the poor in spirit, for theirs is the kingdom of heaven" (Matthew 5:3). Luke's series of four blessings — to the poor, the hungry, those who weep, and those who are hated and excluded — is followed by a set of woes starting, "But woe to you that are rich, for you have received your consolation" (Luke 6:24).

In both cases, the ethical message is a demanding one: "Love your enemies, do good to those who hate you, bless those who curse you, pray for those who abuse you. To him who strikes you on the cheek, offer the other also; and from him who takes away your coat do not withhold even your shirt. Give to everyone who begs from you; and of him who takes away your goods do not ask them again. And as you wish that men would do to you, do so to them" (Luke 6:27–31).

Matthew leads up to his version of these admonitions with a series of radical interpretations of the Torah, in the form, "You have heard that it was said . . . but I say to you . . ." Call it spiritualizing again, but one is to avoid not only evil acts, but also inner states that lead to them. Do not kill, but also do not bear anger. Do not commit adultery, but also do not lust or divorce in order to marry someone else. Do not swear falsely; in fact, do not swear at all. Love not only your friends, but love your enemies as well. In short, "be perfect, as your heavenly Father is perfect" (Matt. 5:48).

This seems impossible, and in the world, probably is. But this is an ethic for God's coming kingdom, and for those who are called to live that Kingdom into existence. Or an "interim ethic," until the Kingdom is fulfilled. Personally, I have always been helped with that last verse by Clarence Jordan's *Cotton Patch Version of Matthew*. He knew that the Greek word for "perfect" also means "complete, mature." "So be mature," he translated. Take everyone into account, as good does. God who makes the sun to rise on the evil and the good, and sends rain on the just and the unjust alike, is mature.[4]

To be mature is to be spiritually disciplined enough not to return evil for evil. Those who are persecuted unjustly will be rewarded in heaven, as were the prophets. Nor is one to seek honor or rewards in this life for being generous or pious. Give generously, but without fanfare. Pray in private, not as a show to others. Do not heap up empty phrases. If you want to be forgiven, forgive others. Pray to the Father of us all for the kingdom to come.

Matthew's version of the prayer Jesus teaches, the "Our Father," has ironically almost been emptied of meaning through liturgical overuse. A visiting minister, before leading it, once stopped to ask, "Tell me: Are you debtors, sinners, or trespassers here?" Because Matthew's version asks forgiveness of debts, Luke's of sins, while the most familiar translation substitutes the word "trespasses." But as a friend once sagely observed, it is also a prayer that is answered to the degree that we fully *mean* what we say, which makes it one worth meditating upon, word by word.

Be persistent and importuning in prayer, Jesus advises: "Ask and it will be given you; seek, and you will find; knock and it will be opened to you" (Luke 6:9; Matt. 7:7). He uses a common rabbinical form of argument, from the lesser to the greater: Who among you, if your child asks for bread, would give the child a stone? If you then, who are evil, know how to give good things to your children, how much more will God give to those who ask. Matthew implies that what God will give is the ability to treat others as one would wish to be treated, while Luke calls it "the Holy Spirit" (Matt. 7:9–12; Luke 11: 9–13).

These two gospels expand on Mark in several other ways. For example, the disciples of John come asking Jesus if he is the One who is to come, or should we wait for another. He does not tell them to wait. He cites what he is doing. Where Mark's Jesus sends only the Twelve out to preach and cast out demons, taking little with them, shaking the dust from their feet where they are not welcomed (Mark 6:7–11), Matthew and Luke expand the mission to seventy disciples.

They also expand how Jesus teaches through parables. Some are just short similes about the Kingdom. It is not only like a tiny mustard seed that grows and becomes a shelter for all the birds of the air. It is also like "leaven which a woman took and hid in three measures of flour, till it was all leavened"(Matt. 13:33; Luke 13:20–21).

The shared Q traditions like this one sometimes speak of God as Sophia/Wisdom. Wisdom sends her prophets to be killed (Luke 11:49–51; Matt. 23:34–36). John the Baptist came eating no bread and drinking no wine; the Human One comes eating and drinking with sinners. Neither is heeded, yet "Wisdom is justified by all her children" (Luke 7:35).

Matthew's particular parables show a characteristic concern with the End Time. The kingdom is like wheat and weeds that are allowed to grow together until the harvest. Like a net cast out that brings in both good fish and bad (Matt. 13). Luke's particular parables are some of the longer and better known in the scriptures. Dante called him "the evangelist of God's tenderness," and many emphasize God's grace and compassion, and encourage such qualities in us.

Take the Parable of the Prodigal Son in Luke 15:11–32. One commentator prefers to call it "The Compassionate Father and His Two Lost Sons."[5] He wants to counter the temptation to read this story on the biblical pattern of the younger son supplanting the elder as the father's favorite, with Christians reading the elder brother as the synagogue and the younger brother as the church. He points out that at the end the father says to the elder, "Son, you are always with me, and all that is mine is yours"(15:31). God's love cannot be earned, neither by stay-at-home dutiful obedience nor by returning home penitent. It simply exists as grace. Both brothers needed to see that, and at the end of the story need to learn how to live in love with one another.

The Parable of the Good Samaritan in Luke 10:29–37 could likewise be retitled today with reference to any despised group, depending upon the audience. Try the Parable of the Good Homosexual with conservatives, or the Parable of the Good Fundamentalist with liberals. Luke places it just after a story he adapted from Mark, in which an expert in Torah asks Jesus what he must do to win eternal life. Jesus asks him what is in the Law, and he summarizes it well: "You shall love the Lord your God with all your heart, and with all your soul, and with all your strength, and with all your mind; and your neighbor as yourself" (Luke 10:27; cf. Deut. 6:4–5 and Lev. 19:18). But then the lawyer asks, "And who is my neighbor?" So Jesus replies with the story of a man robbed, beaten, and left for dead on the road from Jerusalem to Jericho. Fearing contamination from a corpse, but forgetting that life is the highest value, a priest and a Levite both pass by on the other side. A Samaritan stops, shows compassion, binds up the man's wounds, and pays for his care at an inn. So who proved neighbor to man? Asks Jesus. The lawyer answers, "The one who showed mercy." He is told, "Go and do likewise."

Samaritans had never accepted the Jerusalem Temple. By the time Luke and Matthew wrote, of course, it no longer existed. Its priestly leadership, criticized as both corrupt and overly assimilated to Hellenistic and Roman thinking, were the Sadducees, who believed more in the immortality of the soul, as the Greeks did, than in Ezekiel's exilic vision of the resurrection of the dead.

After 70 C.E. the leadership of the Jewish people passed to the synagogue leaders, the "scribes and Pharisees." They believed in God's power to recreate life out of death (look at Spring!). And they set about reinterpreting what it meant to be a Jew without a Temple. Eventually, their leaders were honored with the term "rabbi," meaning master or teacher. They still hoped for a Messiah. When they had to deal with interpreters of Judaism who said that the Messiah had *already* come, before the Temple was destroyed, and would soon come again, you can imagine how most felt: Hah!

I rather like the story about the rabbi and the priest who are discussing these matters. Finally the rabbi says, "We are both just still waiting: you for him to come again, me for him to come. If he gets here in our lifetime, perhaps we could just both agree to ask him a question together: 'Tell me, have you been here *before*?'"

One legacy of the stories of the Passion of Jesus is a persistent temptation of Christians to blame it on the Jews. Behind anti-Semitic passion plays at Oberammergau lie the gospels, I'm afraid. Yet theological and historical analysis of the gospels both make that quite clear that the blame is quite unjustified.

The outline of the story is probably familiar. All four of the gospels portray Jesus as entering Jerusalem in a manner designed to evoke the prophecy of Zechariah (9:9): "Lo, your king comes to you . . . humble and riding on an ass, on a colt the foal of an ass." Matthew, of course, cites the verse and says that it was done "to fulfill what was spoken by the prophet." When the crowd spread their garments before him and hail him with hosannas, Luke has the Pharisees say, "Teacher, rebuke your disciples," and Jesus answer, "I tell you, if these were silent, the very stones would cry out" (Luke 19:39–40).

If this really happened (and it may have), no wonder Jesus was killed. But not by the Jews — by the Romans who were in charge of law and order in Jerusalem, especially at great Jewish festivals like the one celebrating liberation, Passover. The question is, who created this event to fulfill the prophecy?

If it never happened as described, it may have been the evangelists, as prophecy *ex eventu* or "after the fact." Followers of Jesus, as we shall see, after his death used images provided by the Psalms, Isaiah, and the other prophtes to interpret the catastrophe of their hoped-for Messiah having been killed.

Was it Jesus himself who arranged his entry into Jerusalem to fit the prophecies? Despite the gospels, I doubt it. That demands that I be just too cynical. It involves a man coming to the city arranging to "look humble" by the way he enters — and to be acclaimed for doing so.

No, more likely it was his disciples and the crowd. Jesus almost certainly appeared to them as an alternative to Roman oppression and the Temple hierarchy. Perhaps he did predict that a just God would destroy the Temple; or curse a fig tree as a symbol of its unfruitfulness; or create a disturbance within its precincts (Mark 11:12–19; Matt. 21:12–19; Luke 19:39–46). In the outer court, the Court of the Gentiles, merchants changed foreign currency into Temple shekels and sold doves for offerings. "My house shall be called a house of prayer for all the nations," says Jesus, quoting Isaiah 56:7, "but you have made it a den of robbers" (Mark 11:17; cf. Jer. 7:11, Matt. 21:13, Luke 19:46).

The gospels portray the religious leaders as trying to entrap Jesus through his teaching. They ask him if it is lawful to pay taxes to Caesar. He tells them just to look at whose image is on the coin (Mark 12:13–17; Matt. 22:15–22; Luke 20:20–26). What is often forgotten is the radicalism in the second part of his reply. To render to God the things that are God's means to give *everything:* "You shall love the Lord your God with all your heart, and with all your soul, and with all your mind. This is the great and first commandment. And a second is like it, You shall love your neighbor as yourself" (Mark 12:28–34; Matt. 22:34f; Luke 10:25–28).

Jesus no doubt taught in, around, and about Jerusalem. The Q traditions have him lamenting, "O Jerusalem, Jerusalem, killing the prophets and stoning those who are sent to you! How often I would have gathered your children together as a hen gathers her brood under her wings, and you would not!" (Mstt. 23:37–39; Luke 13:34–35). He disparages the wealth of the Temple treasury and those who gave to it out of their abundance when he admires a poor widow for giving all that she has in her tiny gift (Mark 12:41–44; Luke 21:1–4). Matthew includes a chapter of parables ending with the Last Judgment, in which the righteous will be rewarded for having fed the hungry, clothed the naked, and visited the sick: "Truly, I say to you, as you did it to one of the least of these my brethren, you did it to me" (Matt. 25:40).

But it was not the ethical radicalism of Jesus that led to his arrest. In fact, historians argue, his commitment to nonviolence must have been understood, or the Romans would have arrested his followers as well. Some suggest that Judas betrayed Jesus less for money than out of disappointment that he was such a pacifist.[6] But at Passover, the festival of liberation, the authorities could simply not risk disturbances. There had been too many in years past.[7] A summary arrest by the Romans, perhaps at the request of Temple authorities, followed the next morning by execution, is more likely than the complex and contradictory gospel accounts of Jesus being brought before the Sanhedrin, Pilate, Herod, and the crowd. The high priests would have been too busy with Temple rites.

Perhaps it is true, however, that Jesus had anticipated this turn of events. He had been staying in nearby Bethany, where Luke has Mary listen to him while her sister Martha busies herself with hospitality (Luke 10:38–42), and where Mark and Matthew describe an incident in the home of Simon the leper. A woman pours a jar of expensive ointment on his head. The disciples rebuke her, saying it could have been sold and the money used for the poor. Jesus says they will always have the poor, but not always have him; that she has anointed him to prepare him for burial. He then adds that wherever the gospel is preached, "what she has done will be told in memory of her" (Mark 14:3–9; Matt. 26:6–13). Ironically, the woman is never given a name.[8]

Certainly Jesus is portrayed as anticipating his death at the Last Supper as he ate with his disciples. Whether it was truly a Passover seder is debated. It may have been simply a fellowship meal, like others celebrated previously, held just before Passover. Even before the gospels, Paul reports the liturgical tradition that Jesus "took bread, and when he had given thanks, he broke it, and said, 'This is my body which is broken for you. Do this in remembrance of me.' In the same way also the cup, after supper, saying, 'This is the new covenant in my blood. Do this, as often as you drink it, in remembrance of me'" (1 Cor. 11:23–25; Mark 14:22–25; Matt. 26:26–29; Luke 22:15–20; cf. John 6:51c). The gospels follow this with an insistence on a fellowship of equals, in which no one lords it over others, but all serve.

After the meal, they go to the Mount of Olives. Jesus predicts that the disciples will scatter and that Peter will deny him three times before the cock crows. In a nearby place called Gethsemane, he goes off to pray: "Father ... remove this cup from me; nevertheless, not what I will, but what thou wilt." He asks the disciples to pray and watch that they not enter into temptation, but they fall asleep (Mark 14:36–42; Matt. 26:39–46; Luke 22:42–46). This "Agony in the Garden," as tradition calls it, ends with Judas arriving with an armed crowd and identifying Jesus with a kiss.

Pilate washing his hands, in recognition of Jesus being a righteous innocent; the crowd demanding that Barabbas be freed and Jesus killed — are quite unlikely, historically. Within the unreliable trial scenes, however, it is notable how often the basic accusation against Jesus has to do with a threat to destroy the Temple and rebuild it in three days — interpreted, of course, as a reference to his body. And the image of Jesus being mocked by soldiers, crowned with thorns as the "King of the Jews," stripped, with his garments divided by lot—all this becomes an indelible part of the Passion tradition. Several elements, however, are clearly modeled on Psalm 22: "He committed his cause to the Lord; let him deliver him, let him rescue him, for he delights in him!" (Ps. 22:8) and "they divide my garments among them, and for my raiment they cast lots" (Ps. 22:18).

An African, Simon of Cyrene, is made to carry the cross as Jesus is marched to Golgotha, the Place of the Skull, outside the city walls. Two thieves are crucified alongside him. Only Luke, however, has one of them recognize his innocence, ask to be remembered "when you come into your kingly power," and be told, "Today you will be with me in Paradise"(Luke 23:39–43).

Mark and Matthew have Jesus cry out, after three hours on the cross, in Aramaic: "Eli, Eli, lama sabachthani?" "My God, my God, why hast thou forsaken me?" (Ps. 22:1). And for his thirst he is given vinegar to drink (Ps. 69:21), while Luke has him end by quoting Psalm 31:5: "Into thy hand(s) I commit my spirit."

You do not have to be a conventional believer to be moved by the story of the passion, the suffering of the innocent. It is too universal a story to be ignored. As theologian/poet Dorothee Soelle writes:[9]

> He needs you
> that's all there is to it
> without you he's left hanging ...
>
> Help him
> that's what faith is
> he can't bring it about
> his kingdom
> couldn't then couldn't later can't now
> not at any rate without you
> and that is his irresistible appeal.

Resurrections: The Four Easter Stories

A friend once visited the catacombs of Rome. There he found that the most ancient depictions were at eye-level, and showed Jesus as the Good Shepherd. Then he visited some of the most ancient churches aboveground, where the images were higher on the wall, and more often in royal garb. Finally, he noticed that in churches of the high Middle Ages, Jesus typically appeared only at the very top of the wall behind the altar, enthroned in majesty.

"I don't quite know why Jesus climbed the walls," he wrote, "but I suspect that it was because we could no longer stand to look at him eyeball to eyeball."

In the 1950s this man, Con Browne, had been part of Koinonia, the interracial community founded by Clarence Jordan in the Deep South to fight segregation and really live the gospel. Later he helped run the Highlander Center in Tennessee, where Rosa Parks had decided no longer to sit in the back of the bus. After that he and his wife Ora worked for the empowerment of landless peasants in the Philippines. All eyeball to eyeball.

How the Jesus who was crucified for challenging the establishment became the God-Man of an established church is a complex, ironic story that lies beyond our scope here.[1] Yet it begins with stories of his resurrection. Right from the start, however, accounts varied, as did understandings of what it meant to say he had been raised from the dead.

BODY AND SPIRIT

When Paul described the church as "the body of Christ," guided by Christ's spirit to right conduct, he helped to begin one such interpretation. He felt that he himself was a witness to the resurrection of Jesus and had his authorization as an apostle from that fact. But he had never seen Jesus in the flesh either before or after death. Rather he had a vision, "a revelation of Jesus Christ," on the road to Damascus. His vision was a spiritual experience. Not surprisingly, Paul's interpretation of the resurrection involves not a body of flesh, but an imperishable, spiritual body (1 Cor. 15:42–51).

All good skeptics, however, are familiar with the story of "doubting Thomas" (John 20:24–29). Some in the early church were obviously concerned that the resurrection not be interpreted as *merely* spiritual, ghostly, or psychological. "Unless I see in his hands the print of the nails, and place my finger in the mark of the nails, and place my hand in his side, I will not believe," says Thomas. When Jesus appears and gives him the opportunity to do just that, he exclaims, "My Lord and my God!" And Jesus replies, "Have you believed because you have seen me? Blessed are those who have not seen and yet believe."

Tensions between Hebraic and Hellenistic patterns of thought pervade the Christian scriptures, and nowhere more obviously than with regard to human personhood and death. More Hellenistic patterns of thinking, as Paul shows, distinguished between the perishable flesh and the imperishable soul of a person. Resurrection meant the imperishable soul receiving an imperishable body — not one of corruptible flesh. Hebraic understanding took death as the end of human personhood. Just as God breathed spirit into dust and made Adam a living creature, flesh without spirit is only a corpse and a spirit without a body is only a ghost without a real existence. Resurrection meant giving life back to the dead.

During and after the Exile, Hebrew authors begin to use the raising of the dead as a metaphor for Israel's revival and return, like the dry bones in Ezekiel 37. Only within apocalyptic literature, however, do we begin to encounter resurrection as the eschatological act by which God recompenses the dead for their deeds. Written in the second century B.C.E., Daniel 12:1–3 is a classic text: "Many of those who sleep in the dust of the earth shall awake, some to everlasting life, and some to shame and everlasting contempt. And those who are wise shall shine like the brightness of the firmament; and those who turn many to righteousness, like the stars for ever and ever."

The Wisdom of Solomon, written in the first century B.C.E., provides an insightful debate on immortality. Rulers are to be just because God will judge them. But the powerful and ungodly say that life is short, and death is the end. One should enjoy life, even if it means exploiting the weak. "Let us lie in wait for the righteous man, because he is inconvenient to us and opposes our actions; he reproaches us for sins against the law... He professes to have knowledge of God, and... boasts that God is his father . . . Let us condemn him to a shameful death" (Wisd. Of Sol. 2:12–20).

But death is not the end, at least for the righteous. "The souls of the righteous are in the hand of God" (3:1). When the wicked die, they discover that they are to be judged by the righteous one, now exalted as judge in the heavenly court. Acknowledging that he is among the "sons of God" (angels), they admit their guilt and receive the annihilation they had believed in, while the righteous continue in eternal life.[2]

ETERNAL LIFE AND RAISING THE DEAD

In the Hebrew Bible only two figures escape death and are taken up directly into heaven alive: Enoch and Elijah. Elijah and his disciple Elisha also perform prophetic signs or healings that include restoring the dead to life (1 Kings 17:17–24; 2 Kings 4:31–37; 13:20–21).

In the gospel, so does Jesus. Luke tells of him raising the son of a widow in the town of Nain (7:11–17). In all the Synoptic gospels, he is called to raise the daughter of a ruler of a synagogue named Jairus (Mark 5:21–43; Matt. 9:18–26; Luke 8:40–56). He tells the crowd that the girl is not dead but sleeping and tells her to arise. In the Gospel of John, however, Jesus is called to the home of Mary and Martha of Bethany, to raise their brother, Lazarus, who is not merely sleeping, but has been four days dead. When Jesus says, "Your brother will rise again," Martha replies, "I know that he will rise in the resurrection at the last day." Jesus then says, "I am the resurrection and the life; he who believes in me, though he die, yet shall he live, and whoever lives and believes in me shall never die. Do you believe this?" (John 11:23–26).

Jesus' own resurrection was proclaimed from the start from two perspectives. First, in his resurrection a just God vindicates the death of a righteous, innocent man and sets right the injustice and tragedy of his crucifixion. Second, the resurrection proves that Jesus was not merely himself, but a figure with a larger world-historical role—the harbinger of the End Time and the first of those to be raised to eternal life. One can see the evolution in interpretation beginning in the gospels themselves.

MARK: THE EMPTY TOMB

In Mark, the focus is still largely on the vindication of the righteous Son of Man. Jesus three times predicts his own death, saying that the Son of Man must suffer, be killed, and in three days be raised. The centurion present at the cross to certify his death, so that he can be buried, says, "Truly this man was the Son of God!" (But in Luke, only "Certainly this man was innocent!") He is laid in the tomb provided by Joseph of Arimathea and a stone is rolled against the door. On the morning after the Sabbath the women go to anoint the body.

Mark names three women: Mary Magdalene, Mary the mother of James, and Salome. They find the stone rolled back, the tomb empty, and "a young man sitting on the right side, dressed in a white robe." He gives voice to their confusion and confirms the predictions: "Do not be amazed; you seek Jesus of Nazareth, who was crucified. He has risen; he is not here; see the place where they laid him. But go, tell his disciples and Peter that he is going before you to Galilee; there you will see him, as he told you." The original text of Mark then ends by saying, "And they went out and fled from the tomb; for trembling and astonishment had come upon them; and they said nothing to any one, for they were afraid" (Mark 16:8). This is an odd way to end the story. Especially since the written gospel itself demonstrates that the women did speak about what they had seen. They bore witness despite their fear and astonishment. As one feminist interpreter has suggested, Mark may have been using the supposed fear and silence of the women to get his own readers and listeners to get over theirs.[3]

There were originally no post-resurrection appearances in Mark. Unless the appearance of Jesus transfigured on a mountaintop in Galilee with Elijah and Moses, in chapter 9, is a foreshadowing, since the disciples are told not to speak of it "until the Son of Man is raised from the dead." Raised as such, Jesus is to judge his accusers (14:62) and gather his chosen (13:26–27), who will have gained eternal life through living the essence of the Torah (10:17–22). But the abrupt ending at the empty tomb was found unsatisfactory and a "Longer Ending to Mark" was added, perhaps based on what the other gospels had already done.

Here the risen Jesus appears to Mary Magdalene first. But the disciples will not believe her. Then he appears in another form to two of them as they are walking into the country. They report this, but are not believed. Finally, Jesus appears to all eleven as they are eating together, upbraiding them for not believing those who had seen him, telling them to go into the world and preach the gospel: those who believe and are baptized will be saved, those who do not will be condemned. And those who believe will be able to perform signs: casting out demons, speaking in tongues, picking up serpents, and "if they drink any deadly thing, it will not hurt them" (Mark 16:18). (Every year a few fundamentalists die of strychnine poisoning, having taken this as a test of faith they are to perform on themselves!) Then Jesus as Lord is taken up into heaven to sit at God's right hand. This longer ending of Mark is closer to Matthew's theology than it is to the rest of Mark's gospel.

MATTHEW: THE GREAT COMMISSION

Matthew differs from Mark not only in audience and in understanding of Jesus, but in many narrative details about the resurrection. Jewish leaders, concerned that the disciples of Jesus would fabricate a claim that he had risen from the dead, are depicted as placing a guard at the tomb (Matt. 27:62–66). Only two women go to the sepulcher: Mary Magdalene and "the other Mary." There is an earthquake, in which an angel rolls back the stone and sits on it to speak to the women. The women, far from being silent, run "with fear and great joy . . . to tell his disciples. Suddenly Jesus met them and said, 'Greetings!' And they came and took hold of his feet and worshipped him. Then Jesus said to them, 'Do not be afraid; go and tell my brethren to go to Galilee, and there they will see me'" (Matt. 28:8–10).

Angry at Jews who do not believe in the resurrection, Matthew depicts the chief priests as bribing the guards to say "'His disciples came by night and stole him away while we were asleep' . . . and this story has been spread among the Jews to this day" (Matt. 28:15). Jesus does appear to the eleven on a mountaintop in Galilee and gives them what is known as the Great Commission: "All authority in heaven and on earth has been given to me. Go therefore and make disciples of all nations, baptizing them in the name of the Father and of the Son and of the Holy Spirit, teaching them to observe all that I have commanded you; and lo, I am with you always, to the close of the age"(Matt. 28:18–20).

LUKE: THE ROAD TO EMMAUS

Luke, on the other hand, does not have the disciples go to Galilee at all. Jerusalem is the focus of his story, both here and in Acts. The women who had come with him from Galilee go to the tomb and see not one but two men "in dazzling apparel" who ask, "Why do you seek the living among the dead?" and remind them of what Jesus had said in Galilee: that "the Son of man must be delivered into the hands of sinful men, and be crucified, and on the third day rise" (Luke 24:4–7). "Mary Magdalene and Joanna and Mary the mother of James and the other women with them . . . told this to the apostles; but these words seemed to them an idle tale, and they did not believe them" (24:10–11).

> That very day two [followers of Jesus] were going to a village named Emmaus, about seven miles from Jerusalem, and talking with each other about all these things that had happened. While they were talking and discussing together, Jesus himself drew near and went with them. But their eyes were kept from recognizing him. And he said to them, "What is this conversation which you are holding with each other as you walk?" And they stood still, looking sad. Then one of them, named Clepas, answered him, "Are you the only visitor to Jerusalem who does not know the things that have happened there in these days?" And he said to them, "What things?" And they said to him, "Concerning Jesus of Nazareth, who was a prophet mighty in deed and word before God and all the people, and how our chief priests and rulers delivered him to death, and crucified him. But we had hoped that he was the one to redeem Israel. Yes, and besides all this, it is now the third day since this happened. Moreover, some women of our com-

pany amazed us. They were at the tomb early in the morning and did not find his body; and they came back saying that they had even seen a vision of angels, who said that he was alive. Some of those who were with us went to the tomb, and found it just as the women had said; but him they did not see." And he said to them, "O foolish men, and slow of heart to believe all that the prophets have spoken! Was it not necessary that the Christ should suffer these things and enter into glory?" And beginning with Moses and the prophets he interpreted to them in all the scriptures the things concerning himself (Luke 24:13–27).

When they arrive at the village, they invite him to break bread with them. And when he blessed the bread and broke it "their eyes were opened and they recognized him; and he vanished out of their sight. They said to each other, 'Did not our hearts burn within us while he talked to us on the road, while he opened to us the scriptures?' And they rose that same hour and returned to Jerusalem; and they found the eleven gathered together . . . who said, 'The Lord has risen indeed, and has appeared to Simon.' Then they told what had happened on the road, and how he was known to them in the breaking of the bread" (Luke 24:28–35).

"As they were saying this, Jesus himself stood among them. But they were startled and frightened, and supposed that they saw a spirit. And he said to them, '. . . See my hands and my feet, that it is I myself; handle me, and see; for a spirit has not flesh and bones as you see that I have.' And while they still disbelieved for joy, and wondered, he said to them, 'Have you anything here to eat?' They gave him a piece of broiled fish, and he took it and ate before them" (Luke 24:36–43).

"You are the witnesses of these things," Luke's risen Jesus says, "but stay in the city, until you are clothed with power from on high." Then he blesses them and is carried up to heaven. "And they returned to Jerusalem with great joy, and were continually in the temple blessing God" (Luke 24:48–53).

JOHN: DO NOT CLING TO ME

In the Fourth Gospel, only Mary Magdalene goes to the tomb. When she finds the stone removed, she runs to get Peter and John. They find the linen burial cloths lying there, but since "as yet they did not know the scripture, that he must rise from the dead," they simply go home! Weeping, Mary Magdalene sees two angels in white, then turns around and sees Jesus, whom she at first mistakes for the gardener. When he speaks to her, she calls him "Rabboni." "*Noli me tangere*," he says in the Latin text, "Do not hold me, for I have not yet ascended to the Father; but go to my brethren and say to them I am ascending to my Father, to my God and your God" (John 20:17).

That evening he meets the disciples behind closed doors. "Peace be with you. As the Father has sent me, even so I send you" (20:21). Then he breathes on them and says, "Receive the Holy Spirit. If you forgive the sins of any, they are forgiven; if you retain the sins of any, they are retained." Then comes the story of Thomas.

"After this Jesus revealed himself again to the disciples by the Sea of Tiberias" (21:1). Several of the disciples are fishing at night, but catch nothing. At dawn a man on the beach advises them to cast the net on the right. They can't haul it in for the abundance of fish. John says, "It is the Lord!" On shore they eat a breakfast of broiled fish and bread together. Then Jesus asks Peter three times, "Do you love me?" With each assurance he says, "Feed my lambs . . . Tend my sheep . . . Feed my sheep." The gospel ends with a veiled warning to Peter that he also will be crucified, a statement that John (the supposed author) will be allowed to live until he returns, and the closing remark that "there are also many other things which Jesus did; were every one of them to be written, I suppose that the world itself could not contain the books that would be written" (John 21:25).

MULTIPLE INTERPRETATIONS

The world also cannot contain all the possible interpretations of the resurrection. The ancient world equated credibility with multiple witnesses, not just a single account. That's why the early church did not worry about the contradictions. It gave these gospels canonical status because they all helped interpret the Hebraic idea of bodily resurrection within Hellenistic culture, without making the risen Christ a disembodied spirit, disconnected from his specifically Jewish, prophetic, ethical radicalism.

Yet historically it is almost impossible to say what really happened, and perhaps not even helpful to ask. My own guess is that the disciples had scattered. Where two or three gathered, in their grief, they felt the presence of their Master among them. The report reached them that his tomb had been found empty. I decline to indulge in Passover plot speculations on how that happened. Too many people had too many possible motives. Regrouping, they quickly began to interpret all that had happened "according to the scriptures," especially Isaiah and the Psalms. The common assertion was that the resurrections promised at the end of time had begun and God had vindicated his crucified prophet. Soon the Kingdom would come. That good news needed to be proclaimed.

The irony, as Con Browne knew, is that soon Jesus was shoved into the clouds and beyond so that we would not have to be reminded of what he was and what he did. People began to speak of him as Christ, and to say "Christ died on the cross," when it was Jesus who died, while "Christ" named what had lived through the crucifixion.

The crucifixion became a symbol for human beings always trying to nail God down, to define, control, or kill God. Sometimes it is a wonder that God survives the church and its theologians. But the resurrection symbolizes the truth that God will not stay dead, no matter what. Through the centuries, it has helped those saints who have understood its meaning most profoundly to see Christ in other people, eyeball to eyeball. It is not necessary to take the resurrection literally to take it seriously or to hold a form of resurrection faith, Con Browne would say; or to see Christ alive now, in others.

"Is it possible," another friend of mine once asked, "that the real significance of the resurrection might be, not that weakness can become power, but that the only real power is the power born of weakness? ... And the only glory that born of dishonor? Is this possible: that the meek will inherit the earth not because of their meekness but because the highest sovereignty is that born out of meekness? And the highest good that born out of evil?"[4]

Incarnations: The Birth Legends and the Fourth Gospel

Some years ago a group of British theologians caused a stir when they published a collection of essays under the title *The Myth of God Incarnate*. Editor John Hick explained in an interview, "The idea of divine incarnation is a metaphorical (or mythological) idea. Jesus almost certainly did not in fact teach that he was in any sense God."[1]

To say that an idea is a metaphor is hardly to call it meaningless, however. Quite the contrary; meaning comes through connecting one thing with another. Metaphor is the way in which language does that. So not only does all theology rely on metaphor, there is no way to use language to develop meaning *except* through metaphor. And to say that a story includes "myth" is simply to say that it includes story-length metaphors. There is something powerful in the metaphor of crucifixion. When we try to "nail God down" we can kill the meaning of "God." Yet God won't stay dead; creative meaning will rise again. And there is something profound and poignant in saying that God is a red-meat screaming baby, lying helpless and homeless in a cattle trough.

The idea that God could take on flesh was not Hebraic, however. It was a product of Hellenistic culture and its dualism of spirit and flesh. For the Greco-Roman world, a human being could enflesh the divine in any number of ways: as a god who had taken on human form; as the child of a god; by embodying a divine quality, such as Wisdom; by being the child of a god; by being universally, enduringly meaningful.

Nowhere in the Bible is the word "incarnation" used as it was in later Christian theology. The gospels may proclaim Jesus as the Son of God, but none call him God the Son, as did the later doctrine of the Trinity. The earliest gospel, Mark, says nothing about a virgin birth or about Jesus being born in any special way at all. In Mark's theology, Jesus seems to be God's son by adoption, declared at the time of his baptism by John: "Thou art my beloved Son; with thee I am well-pleased" (Mark

1:11). Or in being resurrected. Yet for the other evangelists, Jesus must have been extraordinary from birth.

John has a hymnic prologue that identifies Jesus with the eternal Logos through which God made all things.

Matthew and Luke begin with legends about the birth of Jesus that, while borrowing motifs from both the Bible and Greco-Roman hero stories, function in their gospels as theological prologues. If they point to an idea of incarnation, of God taking on flesh, they do so in rather different ways, however, since they have different ideas of what it means that Jesus was God's son.

Through the melding done by countless Christmas carols, crèches, and pageants, the birth narratives in Matthew and Luke are thoroughly conflated in most minds. Read side by side, however, they are both distinct and contradictory. The Roman Catholic biblical scholar Raymond Brown has done a detailed examination of the texts in his magisterial book *The Birth of the Messiah*.[2]

Neither evangelist was exactly a reporter for the *Bethlehem Star*, having interviewed Mary or the innkeeper. Perhaps not even a scribe who had inherited oral versions of such reports. Both seem to have developed their birth legends to make theological points, patterning their stories on motifs in the Hebrew Bible. Yet the legends they wove have an enduring, mythic meaning.

MATTHEW: THE DREAMERS NAMED JOSEPH

For Matthew, Jesus is "the son of God" in the sense that Psalm 2:7 depicts God as adopting the anointed king: "You are my son; today have I begotten you." He wants to show that Jesus fits all the prophetic criteria to be the Messiah, the anointed one. By being descended from King David and born in Bethlehem, the city of David, for example. Yet how is Jesus descended from David? Through Joseph, "the husband of Mary" (Matt. 1:1–16).

Matthew's "genealogy of Jesus Christ, the son of David, the son of Abraham," is notable for also including several foremothers. Like Mary, all are women of damaged reputation who nonetheless served a divine purpose: forebears of David like Tamar, who disguised herself as a prostitute to have a child by Judah; the prostitute Rahab; and David's Moabite grandmother, Ruth; not to mention "the wife of Uriah," Bathsheba, mother of Solomon the Wise.

Matthew takes the names of Jesus' parents seriously. Probably he knew little else about them. Mary is a form of Miriam, and for Matthew her child is like Moses. Joseph he models on the Joseph in Genesis 37–50, who went down into Egypt and received messages from God through dreams.

So Matthew structures his story around a series of dreams Joseph has. In the first, an angel tells him not to break off his betrothal to Mary. She has conceived without his participation, but by the Holy Spirit, and her son is to be called Yehosua (Joshua; God saves) because he is to save his people from their sins. Matthew adds, in his characteristic fashion, that this took place "in order to fulfill what the Lord had spoken by the prophet: 'Behold, a virgin shall conceive and bear a son, and his name shall be called Emmanuel' (which means, God with us)" (Matt. 1:22–23). Actually, of course, it is Matthew who is fulfilling a verse of Isaiah (7:14), mistranslated in the Greek Septuagint as "virgin" when the Hebrew had said only "young woman," and then about someone hundreds of years before.

In this account, Joseph and Mary live in Bethlehem, not Nazareth, and have a house there. But they have to flee to Egypt, "to fulfill what the Lord had spoken by the prophet: 'Out of Egypt have I called my son'" (Matt. 2:15; Hos. 11:1). In order to move the plot there, Matthew introduces a tale about three magi (not kings) from the East and King Herod, and a second dream that Joseph has.

"Where is he who has been born king of the Jews?" the magi ask in Jerusalem. "For we have seen his star in the East, and have come to worship him." They are directed to Bethlehem according to the prophecy: "And you, O Bethlehem, in the land of Judah, are by no means least among the rulers of Judah; for from you shall come a ruler who will govern my people Israel" (Micah 5:2). Arriving there, the magi go "into the house" to present their gifts of gold, frankincense, and myrrh. "And being warned in a dream not to return to Herod, they departed to their own country by another way" (2:12). Then Joseph has his second dream: "Rise, take the child and his mother, and flee to Egypt." In an echo of the death of the firstborn in the Exodus, Herod has sent soldiers to slaughter the innocent newborn males of the region. This, says Matthew, was also to fulfill "what was spoken by the prophet Jeremiah: 'A voice was heard in Ramah, wailing and loud lamentation, Rachel weeping for her children; she refused to be consoled, because they were no more'" (Matt. 2:18; Jer. 31:15).

When the danger has passed, Joseph has a third dream: "'Rise, take the child and his mother, and go to the land of Israel, for those who sought the child's life are dead.' But when he heard that Archelaus reigned over Judea in place of his father, Herod, he was afraid to go there, and being warned in a dream he withdrew to the district of Galilee. And he went and dwelt in a city called Nazareth, that what was spoken by the prophets might be fulfilled, 'He shall be called a Nazarene'" (Matt. 2:20–23).[3]

Throughout this story, Matthew is proclaiming that Jesus is not merely an inspired man. Joseph is inspired. But Jesus is the fulfillment of the promises given to the inspired prophets. It is in that sense that he is God's son.

LUKE: ANNUNCIATIONS

Luke, on the other hand, wants to show Jesus as son of God in the sense of being a universal savior, for Gentiles as well as Jews, embodying the compassion of God for all humankind. He begins with a short preface to his two-part work (including Acts) suggesting that he has relied on "eyewitnesses." That may be true for some of the events in Acts. But when it comes to the birth of Jesus he is no more a reporter for the *Star* than Matthew. In fact, there is no star in this account, and no magi. Like Matthew, Luke weaves a legend out of motifs from the Hebrew Bible, this time involving a series of angelic annunciations of birth.

Rather than beginning with genealogy, Luke waits to wrap up his legend with one. Not only does it trace Joseph back to David by a very different line, it then goes back not just to Abraham, but to "Adam, the son of God" (Luke 3:38). Jesus is "the son of God" in the same sense.

Perhaps conscious of his gospel as an announcement, Luke structures his story around annunciations of good news. Since the one to "prepare the way" and bear witness to the heavenly announcement of Jesus as

God's son is the Baptist, he starts with an imaginative story of the announcement of John's birth.

John the Baptist's parents are a priest named Zechariah and his wife, Elizabeth. She is barren, and both are advanced in years. The pattern here goes back through Eli and Hannah, parents of the prophet Samuel (1 Sam. 2); back through Manoah and his wife, parents of Samson (Judg. 13); back to Abraham and Sarah (Gen. 18). While at the altar, Zechariah is visited by the announcing angel, Gabriel. In a canticle full of biblical references he is told he and Elizabeth are to have a son (Luke 1:14–17).

Like Samson, this child "shall drink no wine nor strong drink," but be "filled with the Holy Spirit, even from his mother's womb. And he will turn many of the sons of Israel to the Lord their God, and he will go before him in the spirit and power of Elijah, to turn the hearts of the fathers to the children and the disobedient to the wisdom of the just, to make ready for the Lord a people prepared" (Luke 1:14–17).[4]

Six months later Gabriel makes another annunciation to the virgin Mary in Nazareth. "Hail, O favored one, the Lord is with you!" He tells her she will bear a son. "How shall this be, since I have no husband?" she asks. And the angel replies, "The Holy Spirit will come upon you and the power of the Most High will overshadow you; therefore the child to be born will be called holy, the Son of God" (Luke 1:36). "And behold, your kinswoman Elizabeth in her old age has also conceived a son . . . for with God nothing will be impossible." This angelic annunciation is followed by the visitation of Mary to Elizabeth. "And Elizabeth was filled with the Holy Spirit and she exclaimed with a loud cry, 'Blessed are you among women, and blessed is the fruit of your womb!'"

Mary replies with the Magnificat, the first of several poetic canticles in Luke's infancy narratives that entered the liturgy of the church. Based on the Song of Hannah (1 Sam. 2:1–10), it begins, "My soul magnifies the Lord." Mary praises God, who has "scattered the proud in the imagination of their hearts, he has put down the mighty from their thrones, and exalted those of low degree; he has filled the hungry with good things, and the rich he has sent empty away" (Luke 1:46–55). A second such canticle is the Benedictus, recited by Zechariah when his son John is born (Luke 1:67–79).

Luke's familiar account of the birth of Jesus begins with a decree going out from Caesar Augustus, taking Joseph to the city of his fore-bears.[5] An angel announces the birth to the shepherds. The shepherds go to Bethlehem to see and announce what they have heard to others. "But Mary kept all these things and pondered them in her heart" (Luke 2:19). On the eighth day, Jesus is circumcised, his name announced. When they take him to be presented in the Temple, a devout man named Simeon recognizes the child as the Christ and contributes a third liturgical song, the Nunc Dimittis: "Lord, now lettest thou thy servant depart in peace, according to thy word; for mine eyes have seen thy salvation, which thou has prepared in the presence of all peoples, a light for revelation to the Gentiles and for glory to thy people Israel" (Luke 2:29–32 KJV). A prophetess named Anna also sees in the child re-demption for Jerusalem.

Luke then tells the Bible's only story of Jesus as a child. He is twelve and has gone up to Jerusalem with his parents at Passover. They some-how leave without him and go back to find him sitting in the Temple among the teachers, listening and asking questions. When he is berated, he says, "Did you not know that I must be in my Father's house?" "And Jesus increased in wisdom and in stature, and in favor with God and man" (Luke 2:39–52 KJV).

THE GOSPEL OF JOHN:
CHRIST'S SELF-DEFINITIONS

If ever there were a text to argue that all theology is metaphorical, it is the Gospel of John. To be sure, in the synoptic gospels Jesus resorts to metaphors and parables (and actions that function as parables) to speak about the Kingdom. But here Jesus is portrayed with great immediacy as using a series of metaphors and related miraculous stories of para-bolic action to speak about himself and his mission: "I am the bread of life" (6:35); "I am the light of the world" (8:12); "I am the good shep-herd" (10:11); "I am the resurrection and the life" (11:25); "I am the vine, you are the branches" (15:5); "I am the way and the truth and the life. No one comes to the Father except through me" (14:6).

Theological trouble begins when such metaphors are taken too lit-erally. Recognize the metaphorical nature of these statements and even that last one can be read as Jesus saying something like this: "My way of living — with faith, hope and love — is the true way of life, the way to more abundant life. No one can come to God who does not learn the way of forgiveness, humility, and self-sacrifice." Then what is being preached is not dogma or exclusivity, but a deeper and more universal spiritual truth.

John's is sometimes called "the spiritual gospel." Yet some apologists for Christian doctrine have often used it to insist that certain of its metaphors should be dogma. It is often argued, for example, that Jesus either was who he claimed to be here — that is, the argument assumes, the fully divine, unique Son of God; the Incarnate Word, God-himself-in-the-flesh — or else he was an imposter, either deluded or evil or both. Even C. S. Lewis makes such a case. But it is problematic on several counts.

This Fourth Gospel is a highly literary work. Jesus is portrayed here as self-defining in a way that has undoubted immediacy. But it is hard to imagine a first-century Jewish preacher really having much success with such an approach. And it stands in stark contrast with the more historically plausible prophet of the Kingdom in the synoptic gospels. There when Jesus is asked, "Good Teacher, what must I do to inherit eternal life?" the reply is, "Why do you call me good? No one is good but God alone" (Mark 10:17–31; Matt. 19:16–30; Luke 18:18–30).

John himself actually says something similar: "No one has ever seen God" (John 1:18a). An epistle later attributed to the same apostle repeats the same statement and then adds, "if we love one another, God abides in us and his love is perfected in us" (1 John 4:12). The real claim in the gospel is that Jesus is "the only Son, who is close to the Father's heart, who has made [God] known" (John 1:18b).

For John, Jesus comes "from above," from the realm of spirit. But we are all meant to be born again, not of flesh, but of the spirit, and then to follow Jesus on high: "In my Father's house are many rooms; if it were not so, would I have told you that I go to prepare a place for you?" (14:2). John's opening hymn to the Logos, reminiscent of the hymn to the Creator at the beginning of Genesis, says that "the Word was with God, and the Word was God . . . and the Word became flesh and dwelt among us, full of grace and truth; we have beheld his glory, glory as of the only Son from the Father" (1:1–14). But this does not mean that Jesus is identical with God, only that there is in him something of that by which God creates order out of chaos, good out of evil, light out of darkness, love out of hatred.

In him is "the true light that enlightens every man" that came into the world (1:9). This idea was a standard part of Hellenistic thought. The Logos — the word, or mind, or reason — of God, is in part in all things and in creatures. But some conform to it and are more fully realized "children of God" than others. What is proclaimed about Jesus is that this light or logos was complete in him, and though shown forth clearly, was rejected but never overcome; it shines still.

Many parts of John are familiar to us through liturgy. When John the Baptist sees Jesus, he exclaims, "Behold, the Lamb of God who takes away the sins of the world!" (John 1:29). In literary form the gospel is like a series of artfully told sermons, made up of six great miracles and six "I am" statements. The metaphors are carefully related to both the liturgical life of the early Christian community — especially its eucharistic meals and baptism — and to its anticipation of the messianic age to come.

Take the first miracle attributed to Jesus. It takes place at a wedding feast at Cana in Galilee. The wine gives out. His mother tells him, but Jesus is reluctant to help: "My hour has not yet come." There are large jars for water used in purification. He has them filled and turns the water into wine. "Everyone serves the good wine first... but you have kept the good wine until now," the guests tell the bridegroom (John 2:1–11).

The marriage feast, of course, is also a metaphor for the messianic banquet, with Jesus himself the bridegroom. Such theological sophistication, along with a pervasive sense of tension with "the Jews" who have refused the invitation to the feast, has led most scholars to guess that the Gospel of John was written as late as 90 to 110 C.E., probably in a city like Ephesus, where followers of Jesus had been expelled from the synagogues. Another way to account for the anti-Jewish attitudes, however, is with an earlier origin in Palestine, among Gentile and Samaritan Christians.

This evangelist is so conscious of metaphor that when Jesus speaks of the Temple being destroyed and raised after three days, he explains that he meant his body (John 2:13–22). Like the "cleansing of the Temple," this comes very early, during the first of several festival visits to Jerusalem. There Jesus meets a Pharisee, Nicodemus, who acknowledges him as "a teacher come from God." Having just been baptized himself, Jesus says that one must be born anew, "of water and the Spirit" to enter the kingdom of God.

John often adds his own theological commentaries to the self-definitional discourses he invents for Jesus. After the dialogue with Nicodemus, for example, he adds the words: "For God so loved the world that he gave his only Son, that whoever believes in him should not perish but have eternal life" (John 3:16). This is a favorite text for evangelicals. Personally, my own favorite version of it is one that I have been known to mutter at lengthy meetings of liberals: "For God so loved the world that She did *not* send a committee!"

Several beautiful stories are told of encounters between Jesus and women. Wearied and thirsty, he asks a Samaritan woman at Jacob's well for water. She is surprised that a Jew would accept water from a Samaritan. He speaks of offering "living water" that will quench one's thirst forever, prophetically discerns her domestic situation, and tells her that the time is coming and now is, when the place of worship will not matter, because "God is spirit, and those who worship God must worship in spirit and truth" (John 4:7–30).

Some early manuscripts of John also include the story of Jesus and a woman caught in adultery. Asked whether she should be stoned, as the law states, Jesus bends down to write with his finger on the ground. Then he says, "Let him who is without sin among you be the first to throw a stone at her" (John 8:1–11).

Another memorable encounter is set at a purification pool in Jerusalem, where invalids come believing that when the Spirit troubles the water they can be healed. Jesus has asked a man who has been lying there for many years if he wants to be healed. He says he has no one to help him get into the water at the healing moment. Jesus tells him to pick up his pallet and walk. He does (John 5:1–18). Criticized because it is the Sabbath, Jesus replies, "My Father is working still, and I am working," leading into a discourse on how the Son can do nothing on his own authority.

The metaphor "I am the light of the world" is used when he encounters a man blind from birth, and is asked, "Rabbi, who sinned, this man or his parents, that he was born blind?" Jesus replies that it was neither, but that the works of God might be manifest in him, and heals him (9:1–12). The metaphor, "I am the bread of life" is joined to John's version of the feeding of the multitude — the only miracle story that is told in all four gospels.

The metaphor of the vine and branches is embedded in the poignant Farewell Discourses (John 14–16) at the Last Supper. Along with washing his disciples' feet, Jesus gives them a new commandment: to love one another and to abide in his love. If we do this, he will abide in us, as God has abided in him. Finally, he promises that God will send them the Counselor, the Holy Spirit, in his name.

According to church tradition, it is the Holy Spirit that is to help us with understanding and interpreting the scriptures. Perhaps one of the Spirit's functions, then, has to do with helping us to see metaphors for what they are.

Once I recruited a teacher of English to lead a lay course in theology. "But I'm no theologian!" she objected. "Thank God!" I said. "We don't need an expert in dogma. We need someone who can tell the difference between a metaphor and a Sears & Roebuck tire iron!" So she accepted, and did a fine job as a "theologian." So can you!

With a little help from the Spirit, even mortal flesh can be saved from its tendencies toward literalism and led toward a greater wholeness of vision and of life. The error with metaphor, as the inspired prophets understood, easily becomes like the error with idols: it becomes the worship of the part instead of the whole. Dogmatic assertions to the contrary notwithstanding, no single metaphor, myth, or human story will ever fully incarnate for everyone the fullness of the Holy. Yet without metaphor, we would have no way or method of even hinting at an ultimate meaning in life, in spite of the realities of suffering and death. Nor, when we lose sight of it, would we have a way of catching a glimpse again of the Holy, ever-present, even in the midst of such realities.

Salvations: Paul and Rabbinic Judaism

For many people raised in a Christian culture, the epistles of Paul are the hardest part of the Bible to read with an open and objective understanding. In part, this is because so much later Christian theology has been constructed on top of Paul's foundational faith. So it is hard to hear what Paul himself was saying. Without meaning to, we often read Paul's words as though they mean what Augustine, or Luther, or Calvin said they mean. To understand Paul, we need to save him from his followers.

Paul was a Jew. Contrary to popular opinion, he never rejected Judaism or "converted" to Christianity. Raised in a Hellenistic and cosmopolitan culture, he had simply become a Jew with a universal message. For him "salvation" had to do with God's saving work of restoring wholeness to the human family. As a Jew, he had puzzled over the assertion that the God who had redeemed Israel from bondage in Egypt and provided the Torah was the one universal God, the Creator. If that was so, he wondered, what was the role of the other peoples, the Gentiles? The answer, in Paul's view, was the good news that God had sent among the Jews a messiah/savior for *all* humankind, who had been raised from the common fate of humanity, from death to eternal life, and had ushered in the fulfillment of history.

He had a ready-made audience. Many non-Jews in Paul's time had been attracted to Jewish monotheism, and to its high ethical standards, if not all its strange customs — like circumcision and food taboos. Most synagogues in the Hellenistic world had Gentile adherents who were "God-fearers" but not full converts. They were held back not just by circumcision and food regulations. Jews were also subject to periodic persecution for refusing to worship the civic gods. In Hellenistic culture, this seemed stiff-necked and particularistic. Roman law made allowance for this ethnic peculiarity, but it applied only to Jews. When god-fearing Gentiles declined to honor the imperial gods, as Christians later did, persecution followed.

Gentiles were welcome around synagogues because the prophets had written that, in the fulfillment of history, even the Gentiles would leave all their idols behind and come to worship God. For Paul, Christ had made it possible for this to happen — for everyone to inherit the salvation promises of the Creator/Redeemer but without having to convert to Judaism as an ethnic religion. All that was required was the renunciation of idols, adherence to the universal spirit of God's law, and faith that in Christ God's salvation had come into a broken world at last, to restore its wholeness.

Paul has been interpreted in many oppressive ways. There is no need to deny that. Christian liberals have sometimes accused him of betraying the message *of* Jesus by beginning the religion *about* Jesus. Yet Paul was not interested in the historical Jesus who had lived in the flesh and whom he had never known. He was interested in the Christ who had overcome death, and in whose spirit he felt called to a mission beyond Israel, to all nations.

Far from being a betrayal of Jesus, the Christ Paul proclaimed had much in common with the radical Jew of Galilee: a demand that mere outward observance be replaced with inward conviction and faith; an inclusive definition of God's kingdom; and an apocalyptic urgency to his message.[1] Other Jewish followers of Jesus, like Peter, had been reluctant to extend the Jesus movement beyond ethnic Jews unless full conversion to the Law was required. Paul argued for a more universal gospel, in which the good news was that mere outward conformity to ethnic custom or circumcision of the flesh did not matter, only inward spiritual change, through faith in Christ, toward righteousness. Interestingly, it is Jewish, not Christian scholars, who have seen this most clearly.

Jewish scholars like Samuel Sandmel and Daniel Boyarin sifted through centuries of Pauline interpretation to see Paul in the context of first-century Hellenistic Judaism.[2] The man they find is a radical critic of the religious culture he inherited, which was in crisis, but also a religious genius, who never ceased to consider himself a Jew, convinced that the Creator of the universe had chosen Israel for a mission in the world. Convinced further that God had chosen a Jew, Jesus, as the messiah/savior to overcome humiliation and death and begin the final act of salvation history, Paul also argued that "there is neither Jew nor Greek, there is neither slave nor free, there is no male and female; for you are all one in Christ Jesus" (Gal. 3:28). This baptismal formula is central to Paul and helps explain why he so vehemently objected when Judaizers said the baptized needed circumcision as well, or separate table fellowship for Jews and Gentiles.

Understanding the intentions of the real Paul, however, is made more difficult by the way he appears in the Bible. It is rather like the problem of the historical Jesus: there is a good deal of narrative about him that dates from years after his death. There are also words attributed to him that are clearly not his.

The Acts of the Apostles is a narrative that begins with the disciples gathering in Jerusalem following the death of Jesus, and ends with Paul coming to Rome as both an apostle and a prisoner. Composed as the companion volume to Luke's gospel, it tells the story of the early church with a good deal of drama, but it is unreliable as history. Acts describes the eleven electing Matthew to replace Judas, receiving the gift of speaking in tongues at Pentecost, and the early Jerusalem community as holding all material goods in common. It describes the preaching of Peter, early conversions of non-Jews, and a group of Hellenists in the Jerusalem church who, as deacons, take care of the poor and the common table. It describes one of them, Stephen, being martyred. It introduces Saul of Tarsus as a persecutor of the church and describes his "conversion" vision of Christ on the road to Damascus. His work with Barnabas in the Antioch congregation includes uncircumcised Gentiles in the church. A conflict over whether full conversion to the Law, including circumcision, should be required of such followers of "The Way," and whether Jewish followers should extend full table-fellowship to the uncircumcised, has to be resolved through a meeting with leaders of the Jerusalem church. Paul is then shown on his missionary journeys, preaching powerfully in such places as the Areopagus (Hill of Mars) in Athens. There he noticed an altar "to an unknown god," and preached about the God in whom we live and move and have our being, and what this god has now done in raising up a savior (Acts 17). Having taken up a collection for the church at Jerusalem, Paul is arrested there for bringing non-Jews into the Temple. He uses his status as a Roman citizen to appeal to the emperor. Sent by sea as a prisoner, and shipwrecked on Malta on the way, he comes to Rome.

If scholars are cautious in using Acts to reconstruct the life and message of Paul, especially when it overdramatizes or conflicts with his letters, the letters present their own problems. Paul never meant them to become "scripture," of course. Yet when they did, other letters that had been written using his name and authority entered the canon. There are thirteen letters attributed to Paul in the New Testament. Scholars agree on only seven as written by Paul himself: First Thessalonians, First and Second Corinthians, Galatians, Philippians, Philemon, and Romans. Six others use his name: Second Thessalonians, Colossians, Ephesians, plus the so-called Pastoral Epistles, First and Second Timothy, and Titus. The latter clearly reflect a later stage of organizational development in the church, with bishops and elders emerging.

In the Pastorals, women are told to be subordinate to male authorities, to keep silent, and not presume to teach (1 Tim. 2:11–12). There is one remark like this in an authentic letter by Paul (1 Cor. 14:34–35), but it may well be a later interpolation. Certainly there is evidence that the real Paul behaved rather differently and had important women colleagues in his missionary work — Lydia, in whose home a church is founded; Phoebe, who is called a deacon and "a helper of many, and of myself as well"; Priscilla, who preaches in both Rome and Ephesus; among others.

I am not arguing that Paul was an enlightened man on the subject of gender and sexuality. He was a man of his time and culture. But neither can I agree with those who see Paul chiefly as a misogynist and homophobe. Some have suggested, for example, that Paul's "thorn in the flesh" was a repressed homosexual nature that explains why he never married.[3] It is less speculative to agree with Peter Gomes, who as a gay Christian himself argues that the concept of a homosexual *nature* was simply unknown to Paul and to his age. So when he condemns homosexual acts in Romans 1:18–32, what he is reacting to is a Caligula culture of prostitution, pederasty, and same-sex practices by otherwise heterosexual men and women. Paul's ignorance that homosexuality can be something beyond choice, that some people may truly be called by God to love members of their own sex, should not be an excuse for unChristian attitudes toward such forms of love today, however.[4]

Paul wrote his letters largely in response to issues and disputes that had arisen in the churches he had helped to found. Second Corinthians seems to have been edited together out of two or three such separate letters. The exceptions are the shortes and longest letters. Philemon is only a note about a runaway slave; Romans is virtually a treatise, a self-explanation and theological explication from Paul to a Christian community that had sprung up without him, and which he intends to visit. The earliest seems to be First Thessalonians, from around 50 C.E., and the last, Romans, around 60 C.E. Paul died in Rome in the late sixties. In Galatians, the most biographically useful of Paul's letters, he tells us that early in his life he tried to outstrip his Jewish contemporaries in his boundless devotion to traditional practice and was a persecutor of the church before God "was pleased to reveal his Son to me, in order that I might preach him among the Gentiles" (Gal. 1:16).

Jewish scholars have noted that Paul has strong affinities with the Jewish Hellenistic philosopher Philo of Alexandria, who died around 50 C.E. Both tend to think in dualities, while holding what Boyarin calls "an impulse toward the One." In interpreting scripture, they seek the "spiritual," or allegorical sense, rather than doing midrash on the plain sense of the text, as rabbinic Judaism did when it established itself by publishing the Mishnah in the second century C.E. As Sandmel has observed: "There is no trace in either [Paul or Philo] of the rabbinic view that prophecy — God speaking directly to man — had ceased . . . revelation continues into the present. . . . Not what God told our forefathers, but what he continues to tell us even in our day is for [both] the crucial element." Their attitude toward the Bible is not as a repository of communal tradition, but as "a vehicle for individual salvation . . . Both are preoccupied with the question of how the individual can enable his mind (or soul; the words are interchangeable) to triumph over his body. For both of them, man, the mixture of the material and immaterial, plays host to the struggle within him between the enlightened mind and the aggressive senses and passions. Both of them ask similar questions: Will the appetites of the body conquer man's reason? Or will man, through his reason, regiment his bodily desires?"[5]

Paul's personal experience in this regard is famously described in Romans 7. "We know that the law is spiritual," he says, "but I am not: I am carnal, sold under sin. I do not understand my own actions. For what I do is not what I want to do, but I do the very thing I hate . . ." (7:14–15). This is not so much a personal psychological confession as a profound insight about the human condition: "For I do not do the good I want, but the evil I do not want is what I do. Now if I do what I do not want, it is no longer I that do it, but sin which dwells within me" (7:19–20).

We must not read into Paul some subsequent doctrine of original sin, much less total depravity or predestination. But clearly he does have a conception of sin different from that of the rabbis, for whom sin is an action or omission. For Paul it is part of our human condition. So naturally he also has a different concept of salvation, putting the accent not on behavior but on the inner faith that produces righteous behavior. He defines his gospel this way: "It is the saving power of God for everyone who has faith — the Jew first, but the Greek also — because here is revealed God's way of righting wrong, a way that starts from faith and ends in faith; as Scripture says, 'The just shall live by faith'" (Rom. 1:16–17).

More than is often recognized, Paul is concerned about what produces righteousness. He feels that both Greek wisdom and Hebraic law can lead too easily to pride. "Righteousness by faith," faith-righteousness, is a typically Pauline integration of dualities: it is the wisdom of God, and the power of God unto salvation.[6]

Especially since Luther, Protestant readings of this as "justification by faith" have too often been used in caricatures of Jewish and Catholic "works righteousness."

This is unwarranted, just as it is probably unfair of liberals and skeptics to see all Protestant interpretations of "salvation by faith" as degenerating into "salvation by formulaic belief" following an overly emotional conversion. Paul himself avoids formulas. The only verbal confession he commends is that "Jesus is Lord." "If that is on your lips and in your heart is the faith that God raised him from the dead, then you will find salvation," he says (Rom. 10:10).

One of the most sincere Christian souls I have ever known, my friend Con Browne, in joining the interracial Koinonia community, made a special request. Instead of the usual affirmation of Jesus as "Lord and Savior," Con wanted to simply say, "I find Jesus to be instructive."

After due deliberation, the community accepted that as a sufficient affirmation.

Nor is Paul a hellfire-and-brimstone preacher. If he saw a day of judgment coming, he also saw salvation already under way. "For God has not destined us to wrath, but to obtain salvation," he writes (1 Thess. 5:9). The Greek word *orge*, translated as judgment or wrath, is in Paul less Hebraic and personal than impersonal and stoic — the natural consequence of corrupt action. "Do not return evil for evil, but leave it to the *orge* of God"(Rom. 12:19). His analysis is that the immoral and idolaters, those haunted by fear and guilt, are enslaved. If they are subject to the wrath of God, it is because there are consequences to fear and evil; they breed more fear and evil.

Paul does seek to overcome "the flesh," *sarx*, but it is also a mistake to read him as rejecting the human body, *soma*. Flesh is subject to sin and death, but though the body must be guided by the spirit, *pneuma*, it is a good thing. He himself is unmarried. The fulfillment, the *parousia*, is near. There is no good reason to change one's state in the short interim. But he advises husbands and wives to give one another their conjugal rights, and he commends marriage to those who would otherwise burn with frustration, knowing that not everyone is called to a life of chastity. The tension between flesh and spirit is resolved by putting the spirit in charge of the body, speaking of the spiritual *body* we will receive in the resurrection, and of the church as the *body* of Christ.

This stands in contrast to the extreme dualism of the so-called Gnostics, who often saw the body and the material creation itself as simply an evil trap for the soul. Paul portrays the whole body of creation as having been groaning until now in travail like our own, waiting for its spiritual renewal. But now "neither death, nor life, nor angels, nor principalities, nor things present, nor things to come, nor powers, nor height, nor depth, nor anything else in all creation, will be able to separate us from the love of God in Christ Jesus our Lord" (Rom. 8:38–39).

Another term that he repeatedly contrasts with spirit is *nomos*, law. It is not that he opposed the law. It is just that he found in the gift of the Torah no solution to the problem of sin. It only serves to make sins more explicit. So he resisted Judaizing within the church, pointing out that being a real Jew is not a matter of hearing or sharing the Law or of circumcising the flesh; rather "real circumcision is a matter of the heart, spiritual and not literal" (Rom. 2:29). And that is open to everyone. "For in Christ Jesus neither circumcision nor uncircumcision is of any avail, but faith working through love" (Gal. 5:6).

But if he resisted Judaizers, he also resisted those spiritualizers—those who, like the Gnostics, assumed that spiritual knowledge or wisdom was the key to salvation. Paul saw this as a temptation to spiritual pride and a potential source of division between spiritual elites and ordinary believers. It was. In his great hymn to love in 1 Corinthians 13 he points out that now all "our knowledge (*gnosis*) is imperfect, and our prophecy is imperfect . . . Now I know in part; then I shall understand fully, even as I have been fully understood. So faith, hope, and love abide, these three, but the greatest of these is love" (13:9,12–13).

His constant theme to the church is unity of spirit in love, humility, and forbearance. He also recognizes a diversity of gifts within the church and uses the metaphor of the body of Christ having many members as a way of speaking about keeping unity and avoiding envy, dissension or division (Rom. 12; 1 Cor. 12).

It is a deep irony. Paul, who wrote so often for the moment, for particular audiences and conflicts and situations, also wrote with such great immediacy and insight that his works became scriptural and among the most contentiously debated in history. He who reached out to Gentiles, to graft them on to Israel in the name of Jesus, unconsciously contributed to "the parting of the ways"—the split between the growing church and the synagogue. One who could easily have lived with no formulas of belief became the foundation of entire structures of dogmatic theology. An apostle who worked with women as equal coworkers became the authority for ecclesiastical sexism and heterosexism. Yet this is also the Paul who said, "Work out your own salvation in fear and trembling, for God is at work in you" (Phil. 2:12).

Revelations: Women, Gnostics, and the Early Church

You will not find "The Gospel of Mary" in your Bible. It is a fascinating document, however. It comes down to us in a third-century Coptic translation along with a fragment of the Greek original. Here is an excerpt:[1]

> Peter said to Mary [Magdalene], "Sister, we know that the Savior loved you more than the rest of women. Tell us the words of the Savior which you remember—which you know [but] we do not, nor have we heard them." Mary answered and said, "What is hidden from you I will proclaim to you." And she began to speak to them these words: "I," she said, "I saw the Lord in a vision and...He...said to me, 'Blessed are you that you did not waver at the sight of me. For where the mind is, there is the treasure.' I said to him, 'Lord, now does he who sees the vision see it [through] the soul [or] through the spirit?' The Savior answered and said, 'He does not see through the soul nor through the spirit, but the mind which [is] between the two...'"

There is a gap in the document shortly after this. When it resumes Mary is reporting on the progress of the soul ascending and overcoming four powers, the last of which takes seven forms: darkness, desire, ignorance, the excitement of death, the kingdom of the flesh, the foolish wisdom of the flesh, and wrathful wisdom.

> When Mary had said this, she fell silent...But Andrew answered and said to the brethren, "Say what you [wish to] say about what she has said. I at least do not believe that the Savior has said this. For certainly these teachings are strange ideas." Peter answered and spoke concerning these same things. He questioned them about the Savior: "Did he really speak with a woman without our knowledge [and] not openly? Are we to turn about and all listen to her? Did he prefer her to us?"
>
> Then Mary wept and said to Peter, "My brother Peter, what do you

think? Do you think that I thought this up myself in my heart, or that I am lying about the Savior?" Levi answered and said to Peter, "Peter, you have always been hot-tempered. Now I see you contending against the woman like the adversaries. But if the Savior made her worthy, who are you indeed to reject her? Surely the Savior knows her very well. That is why he loved her more than us. Rather let us be ashamed and put on the perfect man and acquire him for ourselves as he commanded us, and preach the gospel, not laying down any other rule or law beyond what the Savior said." ... and they began to go forth [to] proclaim and to preach.

Early Christians had a multitude of revelations, many of them leading to proclamations. Paul had one on the road to Damascus. Women as well as men among them shared prophecy, "knowledge" (*gnosis*), and wisdom. Like most such teachings of early Christian women, however, this one was nearly lost.

In 1945, outside the town of Nag Hammadi in Egypt, a remarkable discovery took place. It consisted not only of "The Gospel of Mary," but also of more than forty other early Christian scriptures, including "The Gospel of Thomas," which resembles the lost Q source that Matthew and Luke drew upon. But none were included in the canon of the New Testament. Inscribed on papyrus and leather-bound in thirteen codices, they constituted the library of a group of so-called Gnostic Christians. Late in the fourth century C.E. they hid them, persecuted by more orthodox Christians. This was after the Emperor Constantine had put the power of the state behind the church efforts to separate "catholic" (universally held) beliefs from "heresy" (self-chosen belief, from the Greek *haeresis*, choice).[5]

The canon of the New Testament was formed as catholic and heretical Christians separated from one another. So far we have touched on eighteen of the twenty-seven "books" finally accepted by the universal church: the four canonical gospels, the Acts of the Apostles, the seven authentic letters of Paul, and the six other letters attributed to him. There are nine others: Hebrews; James; 1 and 2 Peter; 1, 2, and 3 John; Jude; and Revelation (the Apocalypse of John). Before returning to the question of why other revelations were *not* included, let us survey those that were.

While attributed to Paul, the so-called Epistle to the Hebrews was recognized even in antiquity as differing from Paul's mission, style, and theology. Rather than being aimed at Gentiles, it is aimed at Jewish Christians; it is not a letter so much as a homily. Its operative word is "better." Not only is Christianity better than Judaism (something Paul never claimed), because Jesus is better than Moses and the prophets; he is also better than the high priests of the Temple because he is a "priest forever after the order of Melchizedek," having made himself the perfect sacrifice. Christians are also to exemplify a higher form of faith.

The most frequently quoted verses are in chapter 11: "Now faith is the assurance of things hoped for, the conviction of things not seen" (11:1). By faith the hero(in)es of the Hebrew Bible all lived, from Abraham and Sarah on down. "These all died in faith, not having received what was promised, but having seen it and greeted it from afar, and having acknowledged that they were strangers and exiles on earth. For . . . if they had been thinking of that land from which they had gone out, they would have had the opportunity to return. But as it is, they desire a better country, that is, a heavenly one. Therefore God is not ashamed to be their God, for he has prepared for them a city" (Heb. 11:13–16). The exhortation ends:

"Therefore, since we are surrounded by so great a cloud of witnesses, let us also lay aside every weight, and sin which clings so closely, and let us run with perseverance the race that is set before us, looking to Jesus the pioneer and perfecter of our faith, who for the joy that was set before him endured the cross, despising the shame, and is seated at the right hand of the throne of God" (Heb. 12:1–2). Moral aspects of faithful living matter: "Let brotherly love continue. Do not neglect to show hospitality to strangers, for thereby some have entertained angels unawares. Remember those who are in prison, as though in prison with them . . . Let marriage be held in honor among all, and let the marriage be undefiled . . . Keep your life free from love of money . . . Do not be led away by diverse and strange teachings" (Heb. 13:1–5,9).

In his classic book *Two Types of Faith*, Martin Buber showed how the relational Hebrew concept of faith as *enumah*—loyalty, fidelity, mutual trust—among Greek-speaking Christians became a more literal form of faith as *pistis* (related to the Greek word for letter, epistle)—as belief, creed, or teaching.[6] No wonder the Epistle of James has to ask, "But what does it profit, my brethren, if a man says that he has faith but has not works? Can his faith (*pistis,* what he says) save him? If a brother or sister is ill-clad and in lack of daily food, and one of you says to them, 'Go in peace, be warmed and filled,' without giving them the things needed for the body, what does it profit? So faith by itself, if it has no works, is dead" (2:14–17).

Luther hated this. He called James "the straw epistle." He believed in salvation *sola gratia, sola fides, sola scriptura*— only by grace, only by faith, only by scripture, not tested by works.

James is the first of the scriptural letters known as the Catholic (or General) Epistles because, unlike the letters of Paul, they were not addressed to particular local congregations but were designed for wider circulation and attributed to other apostles. What bothers us most in these letters is advice from early (male) Christian elders of this sort: "Be subject for the Lord's sake to every human institution . . . Servants, be submissive to your masters with all respect, not only to the kind and gentle but also to the overbearing . . . Likewise you wives, be submissive to your husbands . . ." (1 Pet. 2:13,18;3:1–2).

Aagh! Certainly the best way to read this is: "against the grain." That means realizing that, despite their anxious male leaders, some early Christians were clearly keeping faith with the idea of a discipleship of equals, with no "master" except God in Christ.

What helped early Christianity grow so rapidly was an egalitarian ethos of mutual concern. Yet they were also persecuted at times, and called "atheists," because they claimed the right Jews had, to be exempt from doing obeisance to the civic gods and deified emperors. Both success *and* persecution caused "the household of God" to come to organize itself more as other households of the time did, under male authority figures.

Pastoral epistles like 1 Timothy had declared that "a bishop must be above reproach, the husband of one wife, temperate, sensible, dignified, hospitable, an apt teacher, no drunkard, not violent but gentle, not quarrelsome, and no lover of money. He must manage his own household well, keeping his children submissive and respectful in every way; for if a man does not know how to manage his own household, how can he care for God's church?" (3:2–5). Such leaders were also to "avoid the godless chatter and contradictions of what is falsely called knowledge (*gnosis*), for by professing it some have missed the mark as regards the faith" (1 Tim. 6:20).

In the General Epistles, a good deal of attention is given to distinguishing true "*gnosis* of God and of Jesus our Lord" (2 Pet. 1:2) from the doctrines of "false prophets [and] ... false teachers among you, who will secretly bring in destructive heresies, even denying the Master who bought [redeemed] them ..." (2 Pet. 2:1). Denying that the Christ, the Messiah, had come was one such heresy: "Beloved, do not believe every spirit, but test the spirits to see whether they are of God; for many false prophets have gone out into the world. By this you know the Spirit of God: every spirit which confesses that Jesus Christ has come in the flesh is of God, and every spirit which does not confess Jesus is not of God. This is the spirit of antichrist ..." (1 John 4:1–3; cf. 2 John 7).

Relatively little is said about the *content* of what the heretics teach, however. Instead, these letters warn against the character and behavior of people like a certain Diotrephes (3 John 9) "who likes to put himself first," and against all who "set up divisions, worldly people, devoid of the Spirit" (Jude 16). Believers are simply exhorted "to contend for the faith which was once for all delivered to the saints" (Jude 3).

These letters were all written late in the first century C.E. Notice, however, that they all claim the authority of men who had known Jesus "in the flesh." Jude and James were said to have been brothers of Jesus; Peter and John, his closest and most beloved disciples. Even before any doctrine of "apostolic succession" solidified, the authority of those who had been eyewitnesses to the ministry and resurrection of Jesus was proving useful in discerning whose prophecies and "revelations" would be considered conducive to the edification of all, and which idiosyncratic and divisive.

No wonder then that the final book of the Bible, Revelation, was also the last to be accepted in the canon. It claims the authority of the apostle John. Yet as late as the fifth century C.E. many regarded that claim with suspicion.

Certainly if a contemporary of Jesus were truly the author, he would have written this letter to the seven churches in the Roman province of Asia as a very old man: it would seem to date from the end of the reign of Domitian (81–96 C.E.). And the message is, shall we say, challenging to understand.

In the face of tribulation, each of the seven churches is given an angelic message: to endure; to weed out licentious heretics; to silence a "Jezebel" who calls herself a prophetess and "is teaching and beguiling my servants to practice immorality and to eat food sacrificed to idols" (Rev. 2:20); to "remember what you received"; to hold fast until Christ comes; and to burn with zeal rather than be comfortable and "lukewarm" (Rev. 1–3).

Then a door opens and a vision of heaven begins. The imagery depends on Hebrew prophets like Ezekiel, Daniel, Isaiah, and Zechariah. Around God's throne are four mythical creatures (like a lion, an ox, a man, and an eagle). Elders fall down before a Lamb, who is the one worthy to open the seven-sealed scroll God holds. When will the New Age come? When the first seals are opened, the creatures beckon forth the so-called four horsemen of the Apocalypse: conquest, war, famine, and death. The fifth and sixth seals reveal the souls of those already martyred for the faith. The redeemed are seen as twelve tribes of twelve thousand each. The Lamb will guide them to springs of living water, and God will wipe away every tear from their eyes (Rev. 7).

"When the Lamb opened the seventh seal, there was silence in heaven for about half an hour" (8:1). Then seven angels blow seven trumpets. Stars and woes fall on Earth. An angel presents a little scroll that the seer eats, finding it both sweet and bitter, as Ezekiel did. The earthly temple is measured and seen destroyed as a seventh trumpet sounds. A woman clothed with the sun is seen in the pangs of birth, as war arises in heaven between a great red serpent, Satan, against Michael and his angels. Two beasts arise on earth, followed by three visions intended as "a call for the endurance of the saints, those who keep the commandments of God and the faith of Jesus." These involve seven angels with seven plagues, seven bowls of God's wrath poured out, and the fall of Babylon (Rome), ending in a Hallelujah chorus in heaven. The angel then announces, "Blessed are those who are invited to the marriage supper of the Lamb." When John falls down before him, "he said to me, 'You must not do that! I am a fellow servant with you and your brethren who hold the testimony of Jesus. Worship God'" (Rev. 19:9).

Satan is bound. Death and Hades give up the dead to be judged by what they had done. Those not written in the book of life are thrown into the lake of fire (Rev. 20:15).

"Then I saw a new heaven and a new earth; for the first heaven and the first earth had passed away ... And I saw the holy city, new Jerusalem ... and I heard a loud voice from the throne saying, 'Behold, the dwelling place of God is with men.' ... 'Behold, I make all things new ... I am the Alpha and the Omega, the beginning and the end'" (Rev. 21:1–5). To those who imagine heaven as an endless church service (and therefore closer to hell), this vision offers this assurance: "And I saw no temple in the city" (Rev. 21:22). Through the middle of the city flows a river, springing from the throne of God and of the Lamb; "also, on either side of the river, the tree of life with its twelve kinds of fruit, yielding its fruit each month, and the leaves of the tree were for the healing of the nations."

Revelation ends with a blessing and a curse: "Blessed are those who wash their robes, that they may have the right to the tree of life and that they may enter the city by the gates. Outside are the dogs and sorcerers and fornicators and murderers and idolaters, and every one who loves and practices falsehood" (22:14). "I warn every one who hears the words of the prophecy of this book: if any one adds to them, God will add to him the plagues described in this book, and if any one takes away from the words of the book of this prophecy, God will take away his share in the tree of life and in the holy city ..." And then the words, "Come, Lord Jesus!" (Rev. 22:18–20).

Quite a revelation! Written to inspire Christian unity in a time of persecution, Revelation has sometimes inspired progressive visionaries like Swedenborg and Blake. After all, its basic vision is one of "no sects in heaven," to use another phrase that rather too easily sounds like hell! Yet its great irony is that it has so often been read by fundamentalists for secret *gnosis* about contemporary events and for clues to the identity of the saved and the damned. In her book *Apocalypse Now and Then: A Feminist Guide to the End of the World*, theologian Catherine Keller shows how apocalyptic visions rather easily become self-serving, self-fulfilling, and destructive prophecies.[7]

The Nag Hammadi documents include not only alternative gospels

(The Gospel of Truth, of Thomas, of Phillip, of the Egyptians, of Mary), but also other revelations that were not accepted as canonical, but deemed Gnostic and heretical: the Apocalypse of Adam, of Paul, of Peter, and two of James; the Apocrypha of John and James; plus extraordinary poems like *The Thunder: Perfect Mind,* spoken in the voice of a feminine divine power:[8]

> For I am the first and the last.
> I am the honored and the scorned one.
> I am the whore and the holy one.
> I am the wife and the virgin . . .
> I am the barren one, and many are her sons . . .
> I am the silence that is incomprehensible . . .
> I am the utterance of my name.

Such revelations, like the so-called Gnostics who produced them, were marginalized for a variety of reasons. Continuity with the whole biblical tradition was one factor. The heretic Marcion, who around 140 C.E. precipitated the first debates over which Christian writings should be considered scriptural, wanted the Hebrew Bible left behind. Marcion saw the creator and lawgiver of the Hebrew Bible as inferior to a higher "God above God," the loving Father of Jesus. Still others saw this higher God as androgynous, and having an aspect as the divine Mother or as Sophia/Wisdom. This cosmic dualism is perhaps the reason that the Christian creed begins, "I believe in *one* God, the Father Almighty, creator of heaven and earth . . ." Not two gods.

Gnostics are easily caricatured: as dualists who rejected the goodness of Creation, who aimed at freeing the soul from its entrapment in flesh; as New Age spiritual elitists, teaching people secret gnosis and esoteric doctrines for pay while promoting their own wisdom. But then so are their orthodox opponents: as male authoritarians, suppressing women's wisdom. The truth is probably more complex. The Gnostic sense that divine wisdom is accessible to all people, and that self-knowledge is a pathway to knowledge of the divine, can be both democratic and profound. Literary critic Harold Bloom argues that the real religion of America is both democratic and Gnostic — whether it expresses itself in transcendentalism, Baptist "soul liberty," the conscience of

Catholic women overruling the hierarchy on birth control, or the new revelation that came to Joseph Smith with the Book of Mormon.[9]

But let us also be fair to those who have chosen to work within the canons of orthodoxy and scripture. Elaine Pagels points out that orthodox Christian theologians like Clement of Alexandria (c. 180 C.E.) could characterize both God and revelation in terms that were startlingly inclusive: "The Word is everything to the child, both father and mother, teacher and nurse . . . The nutriment is the milk of the Father . . . and the Word alone supplies us children with the milk of love, and only those who suck at this breast are truly happy. For this reason, seeking is called sucking; to those infants who seek the Word, the Father's loving breasts supply milk." Clement also insists that "men and women share equally in perfection, and are to receive the same instruction and the same discipline. For the name 'humanity' is common to both men and women; and for us 'in Christ there is neither male nor female.'"[10]

The novelist Mary Gaitskill, in an essay called "Revelation," begins by saying, "I did not have a religious upbringing, and I count that a good thing." Most religion she encountered as a child was cruel. Having "come to Jesus" as a lonely young adult, she began to read the Bible. She was especially drawn to the Book of Revelation. It seemed like a movie. But she could not reconcile the God of Love with the idea of a final judgment. Then she had a revelation herself, in the form of a question: Am I pretending to be more compassionate than God? As Kathleen Norris observes, "The woods are full of people, theologians among them, who are only too happy to tell you that they are indeed more compassionate than God; more open-minded, humane, mature, responsible, and psychologically integrated. Although even in rejecting the Bible, they use it like fundamentalists in reverse-gear, citing Bible verse after Bible verse to prove that God is simply not as nice as they are."[11] Gaitskill chose another path: toward both humility and compassion. Perhaps as Rabbi Heschel put it after the Holocaust, the time has come to recognize that even God needs compassion.

Even if the Bible is only literature, poetry and true religion require this in common, said Thomas Hardy: imaginative compassion. The texts deserve critical thought, to be sure. But so do our own prejudices against the texts.

If you are a skeptic, seeker, and liberal, yet want the Bible to reveal its wisdom to you, only this is required: that you do the texts justice, and look for how the texts themselves can serve justice; that you practice imaginative compassion in your readings; and that you walk humbly in your quest for a liberating wisdom. If this introduction has helped at all, I hope you will keep exploring the Bible, seeking understanding and wisdom.

❧ NOTES ❧

Reasons: Why Bother with the Bible?

1. Harry Emerson Fosdick, *The Modern Use of The Bible* (New York: Macmillan, 1925), p. 3.

2. Christoper G. Raible, *Hymns for the Celebration of Strife* (Boston: UUA, 1972).

3. Isaac Asimov, *Isaac Asimov's Treasury of Humor* (Boston: Houghton Mifflin, 1979).

4. Samuel Longfellow, "Light of Ages and of Nations," #189 in *Singing the Living Tradition* (Boston: Beacon Press, 1993).

5. Jack Miles, *God: A Biography* (New York: Random House, 1996); and *Christ: A Crisis in the Life of God* (New York: Knopf, 2001).

Traditions: Where Does the Bible Come From?

1. Walter Wink, *The Bible in Human Transformation: Toward a New Paradigm for Biblical Study* (Philadelphia: Fortress, 1988); and *Approaching the Gospels Together: A Leader's Guide to Group Gospels Study* (Wallingford, PA: Pendle Hill, 1996).

2. In Islam, by contrast, there *is* a form of such a claim. Mohammed is said to have been unable even to read or write until Allah dictated the Koran to him, word for word, and commanded him to "recite" what he had heard. This is similar to the understanding that prophets in the Bible had about their oracles, but it makes the discussion of sources in the Koran more difficult than has been the case for scholars of the Bible — this despite the fact that Mohammed was quite familiar with the stories of the Hebrew Bible and of Jesus. Needless to say, the Koranic versions of those stories often differ from the Jewish and Christian versions.

3. For a more complete treatment of this analysis, see the brilliantly written book by Richard Elliott Friedman, *Who Wrote the Bible?* (San Francisco: HarperSanFrancisco, 1997).

4. The most likely candidates seem to be Ramses II and his successor, Merinpthah.

5. The literary critic Harold Bloom speculated not only that there was a "Book

of J" composed at the royal court, but that the author/editor of these tales may have been a woman. In fact, there are more tales in J than in E that concern justice for women. See Harold Bloom and David Rosenberg (trans), *The Book of J* (Vintage, 1991), and Friedman, pp. 85–86. Other scholars argue that the J tradition developed through multiple layers of narration and editing, and that no single author/compiler is likely.

6. Richard Elliott Friedman argues that the E materials may have been collected by a member of the Levitical priesthood at the Shiloh sanctuary.

7. This Deuteronomic compilation has long been associated with the perspective and style of the prophet Jeremiah. Friendman argues that D was a single individual: Jeremiah's scribe, Baruch. Again, other scholars believe that multiple people were involved before, during, and after the Exile.

8. Elisabeth Schussler Fiorenza, ed., "Introduction: Transgressing the Canonical Boundaries," *Searching the Scriptures: A Feminist Commentary* (New York: Crossroad Herder, 1994).

Versions: Which Bible Should I Read?

1. The numeration of the Ten Commandments used by Catholics combines what most Protestants consider the first two commandments ("You shall have no other gods before me" and "You shall not make for yourself any idol"). Two separate commandments are then seen in the final injunction against coveting: "You shall not covet your neighbor's wife" and "You shall not covet your neighbor's goods." Traditional Judaism normally does not speak of merely Ten Commandments, or attempt a final reconciliation among the three versions of the Decalogue in Exodus 20, Exodus 34, and Deuteronomy 5. Instead it counts 613 commandments in the whole Torah, made up of 365 prohibitions and 248 positive injunctions.

Interpretations: Reading the Bible to Challenge Oppression

1. Joseph W. Trigg, "Origen," in David Noel Freedman, ed., *Anchor Bible Dictionary* (New York: Doubleday, 1997, 1992).

2. One could do worse than to begin the exploration of what is technically called "hermeneutics" (interpretation theory) by reading a classic such as the one by Paul Ricoeur, *Interpretation Theory: Discourse and the Surplus of Meaning* (Ft. Worth: Texas Christian Press, 1976).

Creations: In the Beginning: Genesis 1 to 11

1. Jon Levenson, *Creation and the Persistence of Evil: The Jewish Drama of Divine Omnipotence* (Princeton, NJ: Princeton University Press, 1994).

2. This is one of two explanations for the Sabbath in the Bible. The other associates the Sabbath with the experience of unrelenting work endured by the Hebrews as slaves in Egypt.

3. Northrop Frye, *The Great Code: The Bible and Literature* (New York and London: Harcourt Brace Jovanovich, 1982), p. 107.

4. Elaine Pagels, *Adam, Eve and the Serpent* (New York: Random House, 1988).

5. Gary A. Anderson, *The Genesis of Perfection: Adam and Eve in Jewish and Christian Imagination* (Louisville, KY: Westminster John Knox, 2001).

6. Ann Schultz, "Doggerel on a Theme by Milton." Published in the *UU World*, 1970s, date uncertain.

7. Alan M. Dershowitz, *The Genesis of Justice: Ten Stories of Biblical Injustice that Led to the Ten Commandments and Modern Law* (New York: Warner Books, 2000).

8. Harold Kushner, *How Good Do We Have to Be?* (Boston: Little Brown, 1996)

9. "The curse of Ham" was cited by defenders of African slavery. Note, however, that Noah's curse is directed to Ham's son Canaan—forebear of the Hebrews rivals in the Promised Land—not toward all Hamites. The Canaanites, by the way, were really Semites, ethnically and linguistically, but they were politically allied, during much of the rivalry, with Egypt.

Generations: Matriarchs, Patriarchs, and Children: Genesis 12 to 50

1. Martin Buber, *Ten Rungs: Hasidic Sayings* (New York: Schocken, 1987).

2. Gerda Lerner, *The Creation of Patriarchy* (Oxford: Oxford University Press, 1986).

3. David Noel Friedman, ed., *The Anchor Bible Dictionary* (New York: Doubleday, 1997), "Circumcision."

4. Woody Allen, "The Scrolls: Two" in *Without Feathers* (New York: Warner, 1976), pp. 26–27.

5. David Bakan, *The Slaughter of the Innocents: A Study of the Battered Child Phenomenon* (San Francisco: Jossey-Bass, 1971).

6. David Bakan, *And They Took Themselves Wives: The Emergence of Patri-archy in Western Civilization* (San Francisco: Harper & Row, 1979).

7. Samuel Terrien, *The Elusive Presence: The Heart of Biblical Theology* (San Francisco: HarperSanFrancisco, 1983).

8. This is one of several biblical stories about the origin of tithing. Another is Abraham's gift to the priest-king, Melchizedek of Salem (Gen. 14). It is also the subject of a good deal of legislation in P and D.

9. Cf. Anita Diamant, *The Red Tent* (New York: St. Martin's, 1998); Phyllis Trible, *Texts of Terror: Literary-Feminist Readings of Biblical Narratives* (Philadelphia: Fortress, 1986); and Naomi M. Hyman, *Biblical Women in the Midrash: A Sourcebook* (Northvale, NJ: Jason Aronson, 1997).

10. Jon D. Levenson, *The Death and Resurrection of the Beloved Son: The Transformation of Child Sacrifice in Judaism and Christianity* (New Haven: Yale, 1993).

Liberations: The Exodus and the Wandering in the Wilderness

1. Michael Walzer, *Exodus and Revolution* (New York: Basic, 1985), 61.

2. James Luther Adams, *The Prophethood of All Believers*, ed. George K. Beach (Boston: Beacon Press), 1986.

Institutions: Judges to Kings, Priests and Early Prophets

1. For an interesting theory about the origins of prophetic speech, based in brain physiology, and of the evolutionary steps that may have contributed to the "end of prophecy," see Julian Jaynes, *The Origin of Consciousness in the Breakdown of the Bicameral Mind* (Boston: Houghton Mifflin, 1977).

2. James Luther Adams, "The Five Smooth Stones of Religious Liberalism," in *On Being Human Religiously* (Boston: Beacon Press, 1976).

3. Or as J. L. Adams put it, "A faith that is not the sister of justice is bound to bring us to grief. It thwarts creation, a divinely given possibility; it robs us of our birthright of freedom in an open universe; it robs the community of the spiritual riches latent in its members; it reduces us to beasts of burden in slavish subservience to a state, a church, or party — to a self-made God."

4. One of three biblical women with that name, starting with Judah's abused daughter-in-law in Genesis 38 and continuing through Absalom's daughter, the niece of this Tamar, in 2 Samuel 14:27.

Exaltations: The Book of Psalms

1. The doxologies are Psalm 41:13; Psalm 72:18–19; Pslm 89:52; Psalm 106:48; and Psalm 150.
2. J. Donald Johnstone, in *Beginning Now* (Boston: UUA, 1970).
3. Rainer Maria Rilke, *Later Poems*, translated by J. B. Leishman (Herfordshire, England: Hogarth Press, 1938).
4. Maurice Samuel, in *The Book of Praise: Dialogues on the Psalms* (with Mark Van Doren), ed. Edith Samuel (New York: John Day, 1975), p. 183.

Frustrations: The Wisdom Literature and Job

1. Another feminine aspect of God was the *Shekinah,* the imminent beauty and presence of God.
2. Elisabeth Schussler-Fiorenza, *Wisdom Ways: Introducing Feminist Biblical Interpretation* (Maryknoll, NY: Orbis, 2001).
3. John Shelby Spong, *Rescuing the Bible from Fundamentalism: A Bishop Rethinks the Meaning of Scripture* (San Francisco: HarperSanFrancisco, 1991).
4. Frederick Buechner, *Wishful Thinking: A Theological ABC* (San Francisco: Harper and Row, 1973).
5. Charles Hartshorne, *Omnipotence and Other Theological Mistakes* (Albany, NY: SUNY Albany, 1984).

Redemptions: The Literary Prophets

1. Richard Wilbur, *New and Collected Poems* (New York: Harcourt Brace Jovanovich, 1988), pp. 182–188.
2. In 1955 the playwrights Jerome Lawrence and Robert E. Lee dramatized the Scopes trial in *Inherit the Wind* ("He that troubleth his own house shall inherit the wind"— Prov. 11:29). Their protest against the intellectual restrictions of the McCarthy period led to the 1960 film starring Spencer Tracy and Frederic March.

Proclamations: Messages of the Kingdom
and the Gospel According to Mark

1. Cf. John Dominic Crossan, *The Historical Jesus: The Life of a Mediterranean Jewish Peasant* (San Francisco: HarperSanFrancisco, 1991); and Wayne A. Meeks, *The First Urban Christians: The Social World of the Apostle Paul* (New Haven: Yale, 1983).

2. Geza Vermes, ed., *The Complete Dead Sea Scrolls in English* (New York: Viking Penguin, 1998).

3. Cf. Brad H. Young, *Jesus the Jewish Theologian* (Peabody, MA: Hendrickson Publishers, 1995).

4. Paula Fredriksen, *Jesus of Nazareth: King of the Jews: A Jewish Life and the Emergence of Christianity* (New York: Vintage, 2000).

5. Josephus goes on: "In his view this was a necessary preliminary if baptism was to be acceptable to God. They must not employ it to gain pardon for whatever sins they committed, but as a consecration of the body implying that the soul was already thoroughly cleansed by right behavior. When others too joined the crowds about him, because they were aroused to the highest degree by his sermons, Herod became alarmed. Eloquence that had so great an effect on mankind might lead to some form of sedition, for it looked as if they would be guided by John in everything that they did. Herod decided therefore that it would be much better to strike first and be rid of him before his work led to an uprising, than to wait for an upheaval, get involved in a difficult situation and see his mistake... John, because of Herod's suspicions, was brought in chains to Machaerus, the stronghold that we have previously mentioned, and there put to death ..." (Josephus *Ant* 18.5.2 §116–19). Trans. in David Noel Freedman, ed., *Anchor Bible Dictionary* (New York: Doubleday, 1997, 1992).

6. Other scholars, of course, hold to the traditional view that Jesus did understand himself as the messiah. See Marcus Borg and N. T. Wright, *The Meaning of Jesus: Two Visions* (San Francisco: HarperSF, 2000).

7. Richard A. Horsley and Neil Asher Silberman, *The Message and the Kingdom: How Jesus and Paul Ignited a Revolution and Transformed the Ancient World* (New York: Grosset/Putnam, 1997).

8. Joanna Dewey, "The Gospel of Mark," in *Searching the Scriptures: A Feminist Commentary*, ed. Elisabeth Schussler Fiorenza (New York: Crossroad Herder, 1998).

Passions: The Teachings and Death of Jesus in Matthew and Luke

1. Rita Nakashima Brock and Rebecca Ann Parker, *Proverbs of Ashes: Violence, Redemptive Suffering, and the Search for What Saves Us* (Boston: Beacon Press, 2001).
2. Philemon 24; Colossians 4:14; 2 Timothy 4:11.
3. Elisabeth Schussler-Fiorenza, *Jesus: Miriam's Child, Sophia's Prophet* (London: Continuum International, 1994).
4. Clarence Jordan, *The Cotton Patch Version of Matthew* (Chicago: Association Press/Follett, 1969).
5. Brad H. Young, "The Compassionate Father and His Two Lost Sons," in *Jesus the Jewish Theologian* (Peabody, MA: Hendrickson, 1995), pp. 143–154.
6. The surname Iscariot may indicate that he had been one of the sicarii, or daggermen, among the Zealots. Only Matthew mentions the bribe as "thirty pieces of silver"—fulfilling a prophecy he found in Zechariah 11:12.
7. King Herod's son and heir, Archelaus, in 6 C.E. put down a disturbance in the Temple at Passover and killed three thousand Jews, according to Josephus. The Roman emperor Augustus removed him from authority as both brutal and ineffective.
8. Cf. Elisabeth Schussler Fiorenza, *In Memory of Her: A Feminist Reconstruction of Christian Origins* (New York: Crossroad, 1985).
9. Dorothee Soelle, *Revolutionary Patience*, trans. by Robert and Rita Kimber (Maryknoll, NY: Orbis Books, 1977).

Resurrections: The Four Easter Stories

1. Paula Fredriksen, *From Jesus to Christ: The Origins of the New Testament Images of Christ* (New Haven: Yale, 2000); and Richard D. Rubenstein, *When Jesus Became God: The Epic Fight over Christ's Divinity in the Last Days of Rome* (New York: Harcourt Brace, 1999).
2. George W. E. Nicklesberg, "Resurrection: Early Judaism and Christianity," in Freedman, David Noel, ed., *The Anchor Bible Dictionary* (New York: Doubleday, 1997, 1992).
3. Joan L. Mitchell, *Beyond Fear and Silence: A Feminist-Literary Approach to the Gospel of Mark* (New York: Continuum, 2001).
4. G. Peter Fleck, *The Mask of Religion* (Buffalo, NY: Prometheus, 1980).

Incarnations: The Birth Legends and the Fourth Gospel

1. The interview appeared in *The Christian Century,* September 21, 1981. See a later version of his perspective in John Hick, *The Metaphor of God Incarnate: Christology in a Pluralistic Age* (Louisville, KY: Westminster John Knox, 1995).

2. Raymond E. Brown, *The Birth of the Messiah: A Commentary on the Infancy Narratives in Matthew and Luke* (Garden City, NY: Doubleday, 1977).

3. It is not at all clear what prophet Matthew is citing here. It is possible that he is playing on a similarity between Nazarene and Nazarite (Samson had been dedicated as a Nazarite, Judges 13:5, 16:17).

4. The Torah reference to Nazarites, who vow to take no wine nor strong drink, is in Number 6:1–4. The reference to turning the hearts of the fathers to the children is from Malachi 4:5–6.

5. It may be true that Jesus was born when Quirinius was governor of Syria, and around the time of the death of Herod (i.e., 6 to 4 B.C.E.), but there is no evidence of a census then. It is also unlikely Joseph would have been asked to go to his ancestral place to register.

Salvations: Paul and Rabbinic Judaism

1. In 2 Corinthians (6:2), Paul quotes Isaiah, "Behold, now is the accepted time; now is the day of salvation" (Isa. 49:8). "In all this, he tells the Romans, "remember how critical the moment is. It is time for you to make out of sleep, for salvation is nearer to us now than it was when first we believed" (Rom. 13:11).

2. Daniel Boyarin, *A Radical Jew: Paul and the Politics of Identity* (Berkeley, CA: University of California Press, 1994); Samuel Sandmel, *The Genius of Paul: A Study in History* (Minneapolis: Augsburg Fortress, 1979).

3. Cf. Bishop John Shelby Spong, *Here I Stand: My Struggle for a Christianity of Integrity, Love and Equality* (San Francisco: HarperSF, 2001).

4. Peter Gomes, *The Good Book* (New York: Morrow, 1996), pp. 139, 158.

5. Sandmel, p. 59.

6. Abiel Abbot Livermore, "The Epistle to the Romans," in *An American Reformation,* ed. Sydney E. Ahlstrom and Jonathan S. Carey (Middletown, CT: Wesleyan Univesity Press, 1985), p. 291.

Revelations: Women, Gnostics, and the Early Church

1. "The Gospel of Mary," trans. George W. MacRae and R. McL. Wilson, in James M. Robinson, ed., *The Nag Hammadi Library in English*, 3rd Edition (San Francisco: Harper & Row, 1988), pp. 525–527.

2. Walter Bauer, *Orthodoxy and Heresy in Earliest Christianity*, trans. Robert Kraft (Philadelphia: Fortress Press, 1971), updated 1991 http://ccat.sas.upenn.edu/~humm/Resources/Bauer/bauer00.htm.

3. Martin Buber, *Two Types of Faith* (New York: Macmillan, 1986).

4. Catherine Keller, *Apocalypse Now and Then: A Feminist Guide to the End of the World* (Boston: Beacon Press, 1996).

5. "The Thunder: Perfect Mind," trans. George W. MacRae, in James M. Robinson, ed., *The Nag Hammadi Library in English*, 3rd Edition (San Francisco: Harper & Row, 1988), pp. 297–298.

6. Harold Bloom, *The American Religion: The Emergence of the Post-Christian Nation* (New York: Simon and Schuster, 1992).

7. Clementinus Alexandrinus, *Paidagogus* 1,6 and 1,4, as quoted in Elaine Pagels, *The Gnostic Gospels* (New York: Random House, 1979), pp. 67–68.

8. Kathleen Norris, *Amazing Grace: A Vocabulary of Faith* (New York: Riverhead Books, 1998), pp. 98–100.

9. Harold Bloom, *American Religion: The Emergence of the Post-Christian Nation* (New York: Simon and Schuster, 1993).

10. Elaine Pagels, *The Gnostic Gospels* (New York: Random House, 1979), pp. 67–68.

11. Kathleen Norris, *Amazing Grace: A Vocabulary of Faith* (New York: Riverhead Books, 1998), pp. 98–100.

❧ ACKNOWLEDGMENTS ❧

My abilities to understand the biblical tradition have been deepened both by those who have taught me and by those who have allowed me to be their teacher. My debt, therefore, is both to my teachers at Harvard Divinity School and to the women and men who have taken classes with me and challenged me to make the Bible relevant to skeptics, seekers, and religious liberals. The great Hebrew Bible scholars G. Ernest Wright and Frank Moore Cross, along with New Testament scholars Helmut Koester and Krister Stendahl introduced me to biblical studies at Harvard Divinity School in the early 1970s. One memorable summer at the Graduate Theological Union in Berkeley I explored the Hebrew Bible further with David Noel Friedman. As a Merrill Fellow at Harvard in the spring of 2002 I had the enormous benefit of studying with both Elisabeth Schüssler-Fiorenza and Jon Levenson. From all of them I gained the courage to introduce others to fresh interpretations and methods of understanding. The probing questions asked in classes taught wherever I have served — in Knoxville, Tennessee; Dallas, Texas; New York City; Berkeley, California; Madison, Wisconsin; and Needham, Massachusetts — all have helped shape this book. So has the encouragement of my able editor, Amy Caldwell. I thank David Minard and Camden Place, a member of the youth group in my Needham congregation, for the maps, and Kathleen McClusky Stahl for her careful copyediting. Above all, I thank my companion of thirty years in exploring and living the themes of the biblical heritage, my beloved wife, the Reverend Gwen Langdoc Buehrens.

❧ INDEX ❧

Printed in the United States
By Bookmasters